DAILY
MEDITATIONS

Data conversion by Databyte Chennai, India

Copyright

Copyright © All rights reserved. No part of this book may be reproduced, stored in a retrieval system, or transmitted in any form or by any means, electronic, mechanical, photocopying, recording, scanning, or otherwise, except as permitted under the publisher, without the prior written permission of the publisher.

ISBN-13: [978] [1 Print Edition CreateSpace]
ISBN-10: [1 Print Edition]
eBook edition

Prosveta S.A – CS30012 – 83601 Fréjus CEDEX (France)

ISBN 978-2-8184-0355-6

original edition: 978-2-8184-0354-9

Omraam Mikhaël Aïvanhov

D A I L Y
MEDITATIONS

2017

P R O S V E T A

Foreword

Every morning, before you do anything else, you must give yourself a few quiet moments of reflection so as to begin your day in peace and harmony, and unite yourself to the Creator by dedicating the new day to Him through prayer, meditation.

It is the beginning that is all-important, for it is then, at the beginning, that new forces are set in motion and given direction. If we want to act wisely and well, we have to begin by casting some light on the situation. You do not look for something or start work in the dark; you start by lighting a lamp so that you can see what you are doing. And you can apply the same principle to every area in life: in order to know what to do and how to do it, you have to switch on the light – in other words, to concentrate and look into yourself. Without this light you will wander in all directions and knock on many different doors, and you will never achieve anything worthwhile.

Our days follow the direction that we give to our first thoughts in the morning, for, depending on whether we are mindful or not, we either clear the way ahead or litter it with all kinds of useless and even dangerous debris. Disciples of initiatic science know how to begin the day so that it may be fruitful and rich in God's grace, and so that they may share that grace with those around them. They understand how important it is to begin the day with one fundamental thought around which all the other thoughts of the day may revolve.

If you keep your sights fixed on a definite goal, a clear orientation, an ideal, all your activities will gradually organize themselves and fall into line in such a way as to contribute to the realization of that ideal. Even the negative or alien thoughts or feelings that attempt to infiltrate you will be deflected and put at the service of the divine world. Yes, even they will be forced to follow the direction you have chosen. In this way, thanks to the fundamental thought that you place in your head and your heart first thing in the morning, your whole day will be recorded in the book of life.

And, since everything we do is recorded, once you have lived one glorious day, one day of eternal life, not only will that day be recorded, not only will it never die, but it will endeavor to get the days that follow to imitate it. Try to live just one day as well as you possibly can, therefore, and it will influence all your days: it will persuade them to listen to its testimony and follow its example, so as to be well balanced, orderly, and harmonious.

Omraam Mikhaël Aïvanhov

Between 1938 and 1985, Omraam Mikhaël Aïvanhov elaborated a spiritual teaching in almost five thousand improvised talks. His words have been preserved in their entirety, as the talks given between 1938 and the early 1960s were taken down in shorthand, and the later ones were recorded on tape and latterly on video.

Many of these recordings have been published in book form by Prosveta, providing a comprehensive guide to the teaching.

GLOSSARY

Definitions of terms as used by the Master Omraam Mikhaël Aïvanhov:

brotherhood: a collectivity governed by a truly cohesive spirit (its members share the common bond of a broad, light-filled consciousness), in which each individual works consciously for the good of all. (Daily Meditations 2007: 24 February)

collectivity [human]: a group of people, usually quite extensive, united by a common interest, a common organization or common sentiments, or living in the same place or country.

collectivity [cosmic]: the totality of beings in the universe, both visible and invisible.

disinterestedness: refers not to a lack of interest but to altruism, an absence of bias motivated by interest or advantage. This is a central part of the Master's philosophy. (A New Dawn, part 2, p. 120)

entities: disincarnate beings, drawn to humans and to nature. They may be either light or dark beings, depending on the quality of the vibrations of the person or place attracting them.

higher self, lower self: must be understood within the context of the Master's teaching concerning the two natures in human beings, the human lower self and the divine higher self, which he calls respectively personality and individuality. (Love and Sexuality, part 2, p. 42)

impersonal: refers not to a coldness of attitude but to the absence of referral to self.

psychic: (adjective – as in 'psychic life / world / bodies, etc.'): refers not to mediumship but to a human being's subtle energy beyond the physical, i.e. heart and mind (and soul, or soul and spirit, according to the context).

spiritualist: refers to anyone who looks at things from a spiritual point of view, whose philosophy of life is based on belief in a spiritual reality. (A New Dawn, part 2, p. 127)

1 January

*O*n New Year's Day in some countries it is traditional for children to get up very early, and to go out and knock on their neighbours' doors. As soon as the door is opened, they offer wishes and blessings so that the whole year may be favourable for the people who live there. I also knew this custom in Bulgaria. On the morning of the first day of January, children were sent to the houses in the neighbourhood to wish everyone a Happy New Year. In their hands they held a small branch of dogwood to which they sometimes tied ribbons, and they had to touch everyone in the house with this branch and wish them well. Because children are pure and innocent, they are thought to bring only good things, and it is important that the year should begin under the auspices of purity and blessings.

These are traditions that should be respected, if not outwardly, at least inwardly. On the first day of the year, you too must think of the first visit you will receive, of the first presence you will welcome within you, and prepare yourself. Make sure that this first visitor is the light, so that your whole year will be filled with light.

2 January

In the *Book of Genesis* it is said that God *'breathed into Adam's nostrils the breath of life'* and that *'man became a living being'*. Thus man's life began as a breath given by God. And it is true that for each human being life begins with an inhalation. As soon as a child leaves the womb of its mother, the first thing it must do in order to become an inhabitant of the earth is to take a breath: it opens its little mouth and cries. Everyone hears it and is happy that everything is fine, it is alive! Because as a result of this inhalation, its lungs fill with air and begin to function. And conversely, when we say that a person has breathed their last breath, everyone understands that they have died.

Breath is both the beginning and the end. Life begins with an inhalation and ends with an exhalation, and between these two moments, a long succession of inhalations and exhalations sustain the life within us. It is important that we be aware and grateful.

3 January

Sunday (the Sun), Monday (the Moon), Tuesday (Mars), Wednesday (Mercury), Thursday (Jupiter), Friday (Venus), Saturday (Saturn): the succession of the seven days of the week corresponds symbolically to a musical arrangement of the planets. And since each day corresponds to a planet, like the planets, they file past the Creator, one after another, singing. They are linked together like beads on an endless rosary, forming a chain whose progression is inscribed in eternity.

If rosaries have such great importance in some religions, it is because they symbolise the unfolding of cosmic forces, the infinite succession of elements and beings. And we too must never forget that we form part of this chain: it is thanks to our conscious awareness of belonging to this infinite progression that we live in unison with cosmic harmony.

4 January

Centres of light must be established throughout the world in order to form a link between heaven and earth. These centres are living conduits through which divine blessings descend for all human beings. Happily, such centres already exist, because without them the earth would already be prey to all the dark and destructive forces.

Do you truly wish to help your family, your country and the entire world? Everywhere you go, you should do everything possible to create these centres of light by means of which the earth enters into contact with heaven. To establish such centres is the most glorious work you can undertake: to help all human souls benefit from your efforts, so that as a result of your work they may receive spiritual nourishment and joy.

5 January

Some days you feel inexplicably rich, happy and at peace, as if you had suddenly received a gift from heaven. But at that moment, do you consider sharing this inner abundance with those who are unhappy and alone? Learn to give some of this wealth, this plenitude that you cannot even contain, and say, 'Dear brothers and sisters throughout the world, what I have received is so magnificent that I wish to share it with you. Take some of this joy, take some of this light.'

When your consciousness is sufficiently developed to think of sharing your happiness with others, not only will your name be inscribed in the registers on high as someone who is intelligent and good, but what you have distributed in this way will be placed in your celestial bank account and, one day, should you need to, you will be able to draw on it. Yes, everything you give in this way remains in your possession. No-one can take it from you, because you have placed it in the reserves on high.

6 January

You would like to discover a method by which you could solve all problems and face all situations, like a key that would open all doors? Well no such method exists. What worked yesterday is no longer effective today, and you must try something different. Yesterday, for example, you read an idea that enabled you to see clearly, or to recover your serenity, but today this idea no longer works, and you must look for something new. In this way, day after day, heaven forces us to advance and to make new discoveries, or we would simply go to sleep.

Every day life presents us with a new situation, a new arrangement of things, a new balance of power and thus new problems to solve. And if yesterday we called on wisdom as the solution, perhaps today it is love, or will-power, or flexibility, or patience that will work. There is always a solution, but in each instance you will need to make the effort to look for it.

7 January

How many travellers speak with wonder of experiences they have had in the desert or on a mountain summit! Faced with the immensity, imbued with the all-pervading silence, they had a revelation, they say, of a time and space different from human time and space. They sensed a presence which is beyond all explanation, but which they recognised without question as something real, as the only reality.

Do we really need exceptional conditions to live such an experience? The truth is that this presence sensed in the midst of silence can be experienced everywhere, wherever we may be. We must silence the discordant voices of our instincts and passions, of our dark and chaotic thoughts and feelings. The silence which then pervades us will be strong enough to project us into another time, another space, where the divine knowledge inscribed in our being since time immemorial is gradually revealed to our consciousness.

8 January

It is only because of the exchanges we make with the world around us that we are able to live. These exchanges are made possible thanks to the powers and entities with which the Creator has populated the universe, which are the many different manifestations of his presence. Even if we cannot see them, these entities are there to help us and support life by means of food, water, air and sunlight.

Thanks to the sacrifice of these entities, thanks to their love and their wish to exchange with us, we are still alive; alive physically, psychically and spiritually. So we must learn to communicate with them, to regard them with respect, as treasured beings who must be approached with care, with delicacy and music... Yes, with music.

9 January

All the conditions for our success and happiness are present, but we do not want to acknowledge them. Why? Because what happens in our lives is seldom what we have imagined or expected. But if our wishes and expectations were realised, we would perhaps be faced with even greater complications and disappointments. Have you thought about this?

Divine wisdom responds to all our requests, but it does so through a series of events whose meaning escapes us. We are not yet sufficiently clairvoyant to interpret the signs which would reveal to us the reasons for these events or encounters in our lives, or for the presence of certain people around us. One day we will understand them certainly, but meanwhile we must trust heaven which has foreseen everything concerning our evolution.

10 January

An idea is not something abstract. An idea is a living being; and a divine idea is a creature which comes down from the world of the spirit, and this living being works on you. As long as you take care of it, as long as you nourish it, this idea moulds you. It shapes you to the point that one day you will succeed in reflecting the sublime world in which it has its origin: the world of archetypes, where these creatures called ideas live. This is why, before accepting an idea, it is so important to be vigilant, lucid, and to examine it carefully to know where it will lead you.

In whatever situation you find yourself, only accept to work for a divine idea; it will give you all the conditions to improve yourself and to make you a citizen of the world in which it lives. It is through ideas that you relate to the celestial regions; they are like bees who bring you the best food for your soul and your spirit.

11 January

What is blood? For Initiatic Science every drop of blood is a quintessence of matter, for it contains the principles of the four elements: earth, water, air and fire.

Blood corresponds to the life circulating in the universe, and within us it is the substance that most closely resembles the light. Blood is this life which St. John, at the beginning of his Gospel, wrote is *'the light of men.'* Now light is the very matter of creation. The *Genesis* account reveals that to create the world God first called light. God said, *'Let there be light!'* It is this light that is condensed in our blood. So we must be very careful and consider it with great respect, realizing that it is the condensed light, condensed divine life. And as the blood always returns to the heart, our life must return to the heart of the universe, the Creator.

12 January

*T*here are all sorts of books which describe how to meditate and what formulas to pronounce during these meditations. I do not deny that these formulas are beautiful, useful and effective. But there are two words which are never mentioned, words which for me are the most powerful of all, words which clarify, which harmonize, and which heal, and these words are 'thank you'. I have tried many methods in my life and have carried out many experiments, but the day I acquired the habit of consciously pronouncing the words 'thank you', I felt I had gained possession of a magic wand capable of transforming everything. If you know how to pronounce them, these words will extend their work to the very marrow of your bones.

Nothing is more important than to thank God, 'Thank you, Lord. I thank you with all my heart, with all my mind, with all my soul and with all my spirit, thank you.' You have all eternity in which to understand and appreciate the value of these words.

13 January

*H*ope, faith and love are three virtues that correspond respectively to form, contents, and meaning. Hope is linked to the form, faith, to the contents, and love to the meaning. The form preserves the contents. The contents bring force, but force has no reason for being without meaning.

When hope is strong, it works on the physical body and has a favorable influence on the stomach and the whole digestive system. If, on the contrary, it is weak or defective, the digestive system as well as the beauty of the body are affected.

Faith, the contents, is linked to force and influences the lungs. We must cultivate faith if we want to receive energies, be fulfilled in our life and be inspired by celestial fragrances.

Finally, if we want our life to take on a vast and deep meaning, love must flow like a spring within us. Without love, life loses its whole meaning, in spite of the knowledge and riches we may acquire. Love is linked to the brain, and whoever wants true intelligence, therefore, must learn to love.

14 January

We can only come into contact with God, the Cosmic Spirit, by coming into contact with the spirit within us, with our higher self. So when you pray to God, you are actually seeking to attain the summit of your being. And if you succeed, you will release a vibration which is so pure and subtle that its diffusion within you will produce the most beneficial transformations. And even if you fail to obtain what you have asked for in your prayers, at least you have gained a few very precious elements.

What gives meaning to prayer? The effort you have made to reach the summit within you. Thanks to this work you set in motion an energy out there, far off and very high, which on reaching you, produces vibrations of extreme subtlety – sounds, perfumes, and colours – that regenerate your entire being.

15 January

*S*omeone might say, 'I want to do good. I have asked God to point me in the right direction, but I always end up where I should not be. Why does He allow me to stray?' It is God's fault, of course, not their own! But has this magnificent being who desires to do good asked themself what they really want? They want an outcome which is easy to achieve, an outcome which does not upset their personal plans, which does not oppose their need for comfort, pleasure, wealth, power and glory. They do not have in mind achieving an outcome that may require much sacrifice. So what can the Lord do with a being who has conceived such a trivial and lazy outcome? So what can God do? He allows them to live their life and do what they want.

A person who truly has a high ideal of justice, kindness, generosity and spares no effort to move towards this ideal, receives some internal guidance about the path to follow. And even if they do not start off on the right path, they will be asked to retrace their steps and get back on track.

16 January

Whatever your suffering and difficulties, do not complain about them to others and do not appear discouraged. On the contrary, try to light the lamps within you. Yes, the worse the situation is, the more you must make the light shine. And do you know what will happen as a result? This light will attract people from every direction, and they will say, 'We would like to help you. What do you need?' And soon you will not know what to do with all these services they want to offer you, simply because of your light.

People believe that their misfortunes can touch the hearts of others, so they talk about and even exaggerate them in the hope of gaining help and relief. But those who are burdened with these tales have only one desire: to flee. Yes, unfortunately it is so: in these cases, it is rare that anyone listens, for only beauty, light and love attract human beings. Therefore, the worse the problem is, the more radiant and joyful you must become.

17 January

*A*ll the mystery of life is contained in our breathing. But life is neither to be confused with the act of breathing nor with air itself. Life has its origins in an element higher than air and for which air is a food: fire. Yes, life originates in fire. Air serves only to feed this fire, and without the presence of air the fire goes out. The lungs merely feed the fire that burns in the heart. The primary cause of life, therefore, is fire, and air, its brother, sustains and enlivens it. When man breathes his last, the fire goes out: the last outbreath extinguishes the fire.

Since it is air that sustains the fire of life, we must pay great attention to the process of respiration. The ability to breathe does not mean everything is fine. No, in most people, even though they are alive and breathing, the process of breathing has become weak, compromised. This is why they must make the effort to work with the breath so as to animate, purify and intensify the life within them.

18 January

*E*ach day of course brings its concerns. But even when you find yourself in great difficulty, or facing danger, try not to be troubled. React by linking yourself to Divine Providence and asking it to send you light. Thanks to this light, you will be able to see more clearly and to establish calm in your heart and mind. It is by this means that you will find positive solutions.

All the dangers and obstacles placed before the human soul can be summarized in two words – fear and darkness – and you must do everything possible to conquer them. There is only one legitimate and acceptable fear that we may tolerate in ourselves, and that is the fear of upsetting the divine order. Anyone who is afraid of poverty, failure, public opinion, or dying from an illness or accident is not yet a disciple. The disciple has one fear only, that of being a false note in the universal harmony.

19 January

*Y*ou are looking for love, and you believe it will come to you from outside, in the form of a being who will be exactly the way you expect them to be: pleasant, good-looking, generous, patient... perfect! Although you yourself are grumpy, selfish and quick-tempered, love must show itself to you in the form of an angel! Well, no, that is not how things happen. The love you will attract will be nothing but a reflection of yourself. You could hold an angel or an archangel in your arms, but if you have not opened yourself to the divine world, you would feel nothing of their splendour. What I am telling you is nothing extraordinary. We can often observe people in daily life who, in spite of the affection of their family and friends, live in great inner solitude and feel completely isolated or even persecuted by the whole world. Well, unfortunately it is not everyone who can feel and appreciate other people's love.

Love is a quality of divine life. That is why you will find true love only if you manage to let this life flow within you, a life that has been purified and illuminated thanks to your spiritual work.

20 January

Dinosaurs were reptiles with four legs that lived on earth millions of years ago, and we now know that birds are the product of their evolution. Over time and with successive transformations, the front legs of these reptiles have become wings. Yes, as unbelievable as it may sound, dinosaurs are the ancestors of birds. How to interpret this evolution? Perhaps among these reptiles there were some who were more enterprising, more daring, more curious who wanted to break free, tearing themselves away from the ground. Some others followed suit, while others, lazy and stubbord, have continued to crawl. Take this interpretation as you want.

Now transpose this phenomenon into the world of humans. Over the course of history there have always been the daring ones who wanted to open new paths, explore new lands. Some followed them, others refused to move, but it is thanks to the bold that humanity progresses. So it is up to each of us to decide whether we will continue to crawl along the ground or if we want to make an effort and take to the air, like a bird, and be free.

21 January

When you experience a desire for something, question yourself about its nature, its quality. Ask yourself what you are going to do to fulfil this desire, to realise it, but also what will you do once you have done so. You wish to be rich? Or course you have the right to be so, but what methods will you use to succeed? And, once rich, what will you do with this wealth? Will it be used for your own satisfaction, or to help those who are in need? And if you desire beauty, once again, you must be vigilant. Do not seek that beauty which turns human hearts upside down and can lead them to despair or crime. Concentrate on spiritual beauty, on that which inspires people and encourages them to better themselves.

The misfortunes of human beings stem from the fact that they bring no moral consideration to bear on their wishes, on their projects. Even when they enter a spiritual teaching, how many think only of finding the means to satisfy their desires!

22 January

We are in the habit of separating the physical plane from the spiritual plane, but the truth is that there is no separation between the two. There is a continuous progression from the physical plane to the etheric plane and beyond this, to the astral, mental, causal, buddhic and atmic planes.*

This progression from the physical plane to the subtle planes takes place in humans through the intermediary of centres and organs which are in a sense, extensions of the organs and centres on the physical plane. We can consider these subtle centres (the solar plexus, the hara centre, the chakras, the aura), to be transformers which enable us to live harmoniously in the physical and spiritual realms at the same time, because there is a continuous coming and going between them. This is true spiritual alchemy: the continuous transformation of physical, dense and opaque matter into fluidic, etheric and spiritual matter, and conversely, the diffusion of this spiritual matter within the physical body, which is then invigorated and regenerated as a result.

* See note and diagram, p. 400 and 401.

*S*tability and all constructive activity depend on unity. Whenever you feel indecisive or scattered within yourself, stop. Meditate, collect yourself, and strive to attain the very centre of your being: your higher self. For it is only around this centre that all the currents running through you will be brought into harmony and, whatever the circumstances, you will sense an equilibrium within you which no shock can disturb.

Balance… nothing is more important than this for our physical and psychic life. And at the same time nothing is more difficult to achieve. It actually takes very little to make us lose our balance and fall! Balance is a moment-to-moment victory over opposing forces and is therefore always at risk. We must learn to control these opposing forces and, in order to do so, we must be clear-sighted, attentive and steadfast.

24 January

If you are really attentive, you will sense that at every important moment of your life (a meeting, a journey, a job, or a decision), an inner voice is there advising you. But you do you not listen to it and you make mistakes. Why don't you listen? Because only noise and clamour attract your attention. In order for you to hear this inner being who speaks to you, it must make a lot of noise; but as it speaks softly, you will not hear it. From now on you must understand that when the higher beings speak to humans, they say only a few words in a voice which is almost imperceptible, a whisper, like a gentle breeze, it is up to us to be attentive.

You sometimes find yourself in difficult situations. Has it ever happened that you say, 'Why did I let myself embark...? There was something there, that warned me, but that voice was so faint...' Well, draw the conclusion: in future beware of voices that speak a great deal and very loudly in order to fool you, and try rather to listen to the soft voice from heaven that wants you to avoid unnecessary suffering.

25 January

A thought is a living being, and in the region where it dwells, with the subtle materials of which it is formed, possesses great powers. Ignorance of this truth is the cause of many difficulties and hardships for human beings. They fail to see, they do not sense that their thought is at work, building up or destroying, and so they allow themselves to think no matter what, no matter how and then they are surprised at what happens to them.

Each of our thoughts is a living entity, which is why you must watch yourself to ensure that you project only the best thoughts, thoughts filled with love, goodness, light and peace. This is where true knowledge begins, with the awareness that a thought is a real being. Even if we can neither see them nor hear them, let alone touch them, all thoughts however weak or insignificant they may be, behave like living creatures.

*H*uman beings too often identify love with pleasure, and this is why their love becomes poison in the end. To save their love they need to become aware of the work they can do with it and devote it to God by saying, 'Lord, I devote these energies I feel bubbling up inside me to serving your glory and to the coming of your Kingdom.'

Of course only a few men and women will accept this idea of love many will even find it ridiculous. They think their feelings and emotions concern only themselves and have nothing to do with Heaven. But if they do not concern Heaven, it is hell that comes to get involved and have its say. When someone claims, 'My love concerns only me,' this 'me', who seeks only to enjoy pleasure in a selfish way, is already on the road to hell. Why do men and women exclude Heaven from their love? It seems as if they are ashamed and are trying to hide from it. But they feel no shame when it comes to hell. Well, then they should not complain if there comes a time when they have the feeling of living hell.

27 January

*H*eaven judges people only by what they are capable of giving with the means at their disposal. We meet people in life who are truly deprived: they were born into impoverished families where they have been ill-treated and raised with the worst possible examples. They have poor health and have had little schooling and one would think that there is nothing to expect from them. And yet, through sustained effort and unwavering conviction, they have managed to triumph over their circumstances and to achieve what others, far more privileged than they, have not been able to achieve.

Well, this is what heaven looks at when it sends us to earth: what we succeed in doing with the faculties we are given and the conditions we have to work in. For life is so rich in possibilities that each of us can always find ways to improve ourselves and to enrich ourselves spiritually.

28 January

To what extent is man free? Thinkers and theologians have discussed this question for centuries without reaching agreement; because they are not asking the correct question. Freedom is not a condition that is either given or not, once and for all, to humanity. Instead of asking, 'Am I free?' each of us must understand that our present life is the consequence of our past life, and it is impossible to return to the past and change it. We must endure the past and assimilate it, and this is what we are doing in the present life. But as for the future, we are free, because only the present gives us the potential to create the future we wish for.

This is how to ask the question about freedom. Knowing that from now on we are able to determine our future; we are preparing ourselves to become more and more the masters of our destiny, so we no longer endure the present, we shape it.

29 January

*B*etween air and fire there is a kind of complementarity. To work with fire, one must also know air. It tempers fire, but because it is always moving, it also brings a certain freshness: when it is hot, we wish for air.

These relationships between air and fire are also found in our psychic life. We are travellers journeying through space and, in order to fulfil our destiny, we need fire and air, or heat and cold. We have fire within us: we come into the world carrying our stove and its fuel, so that we can heat ourselves; for the journey is long and outside symbolically it is cold. This cold that rules outside us is air, and thanks to it we can regulate the temperature. Fire one may say is love, and air is wisdom. Love is within us, whereas wisdom is outside us so that we can study it, contemplate it, and use it to regulate our inner fire.

30 January

As we set about discovering the meaning of life, we must not begin by questioning the existence of God. In fact, we must do the exact opposite. If we give greater and richer meaning to every moment of our life, the existence of God will be obvious.

God is life, the fullness of life, and in order to feel his presence we must come alive and discover that everything around us is also alive: the earth is alive, water and air are alive, fire and light are alive! What can a dead person feel? No matter what you give them, they will not react, because their life has gone and they can feel nothing. In order to experience sensations, we must be alive. You will say you already know this. Yes, theoretically, everyone knows it. But this is not enough, which is why everywhere we go we meet so many walking corpses, who wonder what they are doing on this earth. May they eventually decide to revive life within themselves.

31 January

*I*f I did not believe that you were inhabited by the Divinity, that you are divinities, I would perhaps have become discouraged and abandoned everything long ago. It is for the Divinity that dwells within you that I continue. And so, when I adopt an attitude towards certain people, others who are well intentioned, reproach me. They say, 'But why do you not see this person as they really are? You receive him and you trust him. Be careful, for they will create problems for you.' In reality I see quite clearly, but I know what I am doing, and it is they who do not know.

I know that by showing them my understanding, my trust, I can arouse in some people the need to improve, as I address the divinity that is within them. I use this teaching method consciously. I know the risks, and if nothing good comes out of them, I obviously think it's a shame, but I'm not devastated or discouraged.

1 February

Someone who has won a few victories over their bad habits: laziness, anger, jealousy, sensuality should not feel proud of themselves. If they start to think, 'Oh! I am strong!' their lower nature will respond and prepare traps; and these traps are so subtle that they will fall into them right away, without any doubt.

You do not yet know the tricks of the lower nature. It is when you are the most confident that it takes the upper hand and succeeds in surprising you the most. You must remain humble and do not delude yourself about the few small results that you have obtained. Realize that the satisfaction of having won a victory exposes you to danger, and tell yourself, 'Who knows what awaits me now? It is too early to triumph.' Don't just be alert, ask beings of light to continue to support you in your efforts.

2 February

*A*lthough they claim to practice a religion or follow a spiritual teaching, many people live in uncertainty and doubt. Thus they continue to introduce division within themselves and eventually falter. Look at what the woodcutter does when he is not able to cut down a tree, armed with just his axe: in order to bring the tree down he drives a wedge into the cut he makes at the base of the trunk. Unknowingly, those who have doubts allow little wedges to be driven into themselves, and thanks to all the axes in existence – outer, and especially inner difficulties – they are then quickly brought down.

On the path of light to which you are committed, if doubt or uncertainty are able to enter your trunk, your psychic and spiritual energies begin to escape. Therefore, any time you feel threatened, go deep inside yourself and tell yourself, 'Right now my vision is obscured, but I continue to put my faith in good, in the light, I will act with honesty and courage.' If you can stay in that state of mind, the trunk of your inner tree will leap boldly towards heaven.

3 February

Let us say you have met a person for whom you feel sympathy, friendship, and even love... and these sentiments are reciprocated. If you want them to last, you must learn to temper their manifestations. A lack of moderation is dangerous, even in the best circumstances. Of course, we are immediately tempted to give free rein to our affection, letters, meetings, gifts, kisses, and so on. But it is too much. Right away we have had our fill, as if we have eaten too much, and at the first opportunity we reject each other.

To sustain harmonious relationships throughout our lives with those we appreciate, those we love, we must be measured; otherwise, even with the best people in the world, they cannot last. These are psychological subtleties you must understand in order to avoid disappointment.

4 February

The word Bible means book. But the true Bible, the real book, is the book of living nature. That is to say, the universe created by God, and also the human being, that he made in the image of this universe and into whom he breathed his spirit. All sacred books have their origins in this great book, and each presents only a few fragments of it. The book of nature alone is complete and indestructible, and if you have not learned to read it, you can spend your entire life reading the Bible and you will still understand very little of it.

Fanatics may brandish the Bible, the Koran or other sacred texts but, even if they are divinely inspired, these books can never replace the book in which the Creator has inscribed everything: the human being. This book possesses what neither the Bible nor the other sacred books possess: a soul and a spirit which are alive and eternal.

5 February

*S*ome spiritualists claim that we must become detached from the material world in order to come closer to the spirit. In doing so, they have even gone to the point of disregarding hygiene, aesthetics, and simple common sense. As if the spirit could be happy living in filth, ugliness and insanity!

You may say thatit is by choice that some ascetics have chosen to live in the worst conditions. I know, but are they certain they are actually any closer to the spirit? To seek hardships and difficulties is, in fact, a sign of pathalogical abnormality. There are those who take pleasure in suffering and mistreatment, just as others wallow in pleasures. This is no proof of spirituality. Where the spirit manifests, life takes on the most reasonable and harmonious forms.

6 February

So many people enjoy delving into the lives of others in order to find a few hidden faults in behaviour which they can talk about wherever they go. On their faces we read only doubt and distrust, and their suspicious glances see dishonesty and betrayal even where there are none. What is the point of acting like this? Not only do these people sow discord, but they become so disagreeable! With their sombre expressions, they themselves begin to look like criminals.

That is what is extraordinary: those who are so distrustful and who imagine themselves models of justice and honesty finally manifest on their own faces traces of the faults and vices they are so busy detecting in others. But if you look at the face of those who seek to discover people's hidden qualities and virtues: they gradually come to reflect the light of divine splendour.

7 February

*I*n order to transcend the limits of their consciousness, a disciple of initiatic science must learn to project themself to great heights, to the sublime Being who embraces and nourishes every creature. The disciple seeks to know how this Being envisions the destiny of mankind, what plans he has in mind for the disciple's own evolution, not just in the near future, but more importantly in the distant future. And through striving to draw closer and closer to this immense, luminous and perfect Being that the disciple is able to detach themself. A transformation takes place within them, in their subconscious, in their consciousness, and in their superconsciousness, and what they then feel and experience is indescribable.

This practice is one of the most beneficial for the disciple: by devoting themselves to it every day, they distance themselves from their limited ego and dissolve into this ocean of light which is God. It is here that they receive true knowledge and discover freedom.

8 February

Many Christian and Jewish religions have gradually banned animal sacrifices, and cows and sheep are no longer burned on their altars. However, this idea of sacrifice by fire is still present in all religions, as not only candles but also incense are burned before the altar.

Incense is matter given to the fire to be consumed, and in the process it releases a fragrance which pervades the atmosphere. On its own, burning incense has meaning only if the believer understands that this act is a reflection of psychic processes. What they themselves have to sacrifice, are their weaknesses, faults, vices, which are like a thick, murky substance. This substance must be transformed by delivering it to the divine fire, so that their soul emits fragrant emanations. Otherwise, why bother? Spreading the pleasant perfume of incense to the nostrils of the assistants, that's fine, but it is not enough.

9 February

On the grounds that charlatans and crooks can pass themselves off as initates, many people systematically reject the idea of a spiritual master. But what odd reasoning! Do these people stop listening to music because some musicians compose awful sounds? Do they no longer visit galleries because the artwork of some artists is just daubs of paint? Do they no longer read books because some authors write nonsense? Why then this lack of logic?

The truth is that to listen to music, to seek out works of art or to read books is quite easy, whereas to undertake the path of the spiritual life, to accept a discipline in life and to do exercises every day requires great time and effort. Then are not all these people, who reject the idea of a spiritual master simply lazy, finding every excuse to refuse the light of a true guide, and to avoid making an effort?

10 February

*I*f you are insignificant and little known in society, you are powerless to intervene in the affairs of state. To be able to do so, you must try to reach the summit, where the king or president is to be found, and become their minister. Then, yes, you have the power, because you have reached the zenith or the focal point. As long as you remain below, or on the periphery, no-one listens to you and you do not achieve much.

This law also applies in the spiritual realm. Until you succeed in reaching the centre or the summit within you, that is to say your spirit, you can achieve certain things, of course, but you are not truly in charge of anything. Whereas once you manage to connect with your spirit, you become the master, because this centre affords you all possibilities. So, stop being concerned with the periphery down below where you will be limited. Work to reach the spirit within you, without worrying about the time it will take.

11 February

*O*nly those who understand, first and foremost, that they are a child of the heavenly Father and the divine Mother can progress on the path of initiation. They do not reason like these so-called philosophers or scientists who find the idea of God absurd, out-of-date and believe they are being intelligent and showing a free mind by leaving God, in order to live an independent life away from him. They think, 'To be a son of God, a daughter of God what nonsense! We are adults.' Well, no, they are not adults but recalcitrant children.

The true adult, in the initiatic sense, never leaves his celestial parents to seek independence. Only unconscious, ignorant children demand independence and freedom far from the Lord. And then they wonder why they suffer, both physically and psychically. This is not hard to understand; when someone separates from God, they are no longer nourished, protected, supported or educated. All those who have left their divine parents are beset by troubles and distress. So, embrace your celestial Father and Mother, and trust them wholeheartedly.

12 February

*H*uman history is a succession of changes. Nothing remains static, for life is in perpetual movement. We would like to believe that this movement always represents progress and moves in the direction of evolution. But, unfortunately, we cannot help observing that sometimes there are regressions.

But evolution or regression, nothing remains the same; generations of human beings succeed one another and, even if in some countries the changes take place more slowly than in others, or are moving in the wrong direction, when the conditions lend themselves, no one can prevent events from taking a favourable turn. The first currents are emitted by luminous spirits of the invisible world, and the beings who are ready to capture these currents become their conductors. And when the time comes, the changes will also be accepted by the entire society.

13 February

*I*t is written in the Book of Genesis that on the sixth day, after having separated the earth from the waters and created the sun, moon, stars, plants and animals, God said, *'Let us make humankind in our image, according to our likeness'*.

The universe is the body of God, a body which he animates with his spirit. In the same way, the human being has a body which is a reflection of the universe, and the spirit which animates this body is a spark from the divine Spirit. So God is not a monarch, as some might see him, who reigns far from view in some inaccessible place in the farthest reaches of heaven. Undoubtedly there is no being who is more impenetrable or imperceptible, but at the same time he is the closest, for he is inside us. Thus, there is a great work for us to carry out so that we may sense and bring to life this presence within us. Nothing is more precious than the sensation that we are inhabited by God and then, whatever happens, nothing can shake our conviction.

14 February

We see that more and more people are taking an interest in finance and the economy, and have become experts in the field. At least, that is what they believe! But in reality, if they truly understood economic and financial matters, they would have first learned how to look after the spiritual riches they receive from heaven; they would understand how to preserve them and make them grow.

Any ignoramus knows that if they do not make their capital grow, after a while there will be nothing left, because capital which does not yield a return is quickly dissipated. But where the spiritual realm is concerned, even the most educated become poor: they forget that light, warmth and inner wealth are quickly exhausted if they do not work each day to increase them. And how to increase them? Through prayer, meditation and exercises. By connecting each day with the inexhaustible Source of life, the divine Source, we continually renew the energies that enable us to accomplish our task.

15 February

*I*n its original meaning, the word 'charity', which like faith and hope, is a theological virtue (that is to say which has God as a purpose), refers to the love of human beings for God, which of necessity calls for neighbourly love. Unfortunately, this word 'charity' has lost its sublime significance over time, and what we now call 'charity' is expressed in actions which may not be accompanied by any feelings of true love. Many people 'do charitable works' because their church and family have taught them that they must give to the poor, help the unfortunate, and so on.

Charity is thus often the product of a narrow education, and has nothing to do with goodness. How many 'charitable' people poison the lives of their family and friends! There are many of these charitable people, but we meet very few who are truly good. Christians must make the effort to rediscover the original meaning of the word 'charity', which means 'love', for those who claim to love God must also love him through their neighbours.

16 February

God is not there to fulfil people's desire for ease, tranquillity and well-being. He is only concerned with what will make them grow. But that is what human beings do not really understand. When they suffer, they pray to the Lord... This is very good, prayer can help them, but only if they know how it is to be used, for what purpose, and when. Otherwise they will not feel their prayers have been answered.

So, when you are suffering, do not ask God to free you from this suffering, but to help you endure it so that you may extract every benefit from it. Suffering exists not for the purpose of hurting us, but to teach us where genuine good is to be found, and thus to make us stronger, more intelligent and more vibrant. Repeat to yourself every day that thanks to suffering you will gain great wisdom. And know that in talking to you like this, I am not minimising or underestimating your suffering; know that I am also talking to myself, because all human beings without exception need to educate and perfect themselves.

17 February

No other failing gives rise to as much disappointment and misfortune to human beings, as the stubborn defence of certain beliefs and points of view, without testing their validity. People persist in thinking they are right, even when all sorts of events in their daily lives prove the opposite. How can they accept such contradictions? It is the events of life that should prove that they are true and not and not their imagination, their tastes or their preferences.

I have given you many criteria to enlighten you, to guide you! The most important is this one: before reaching a decision on any matter whatsoever, try to identify what it is in yourself that urges you to go in one direction rather than another. Are your motives honest and disinterested? If not, watch out, because you are exposing yourself to great disillusionment.

18 February

*O*ur life is simply a succession of encounters, of contacts with objects, places, situations, human beings and other creatures. Everyone wants to experience and know. Why? Because they think that with this newly acquired knowledge they will gain something. That is true, but be careful, or you run the risk that the opposite may happen.

The fly looks at the spider's web with great curiosity. It wants to know what it is. It has no idea that in this magnificent web of threads lurks the very cunning creature who used all its talents to spin it, and so the fly ventures in and makes the acquaintance of the spider. The artist who conceived this trap is of course delighted, but for the fly it is the end. Well, life is full of spider's webs and traps like this, waiting for the curious and unwary who think they can venture forth without being aware of the dangers.

19 February

*G*enerally people refer to 'miracles' as phenomena they believe defy or negate the laws of nature. Well, no such phenomena exist; everything obeys the laws of nature. And if people speak of miracles, it is because they do not know the laws that would explain them. There are certain phenomena that are exceptional because the people capable of producing them are very rare, but miracles, as most believers imagine them, simply do not exist.

Even things that are truly extraordinary are natural; nothing is 'supernatural'. And the explanation is simple; the gradations in nature are infinite, from the most material to the most subtle, and the sublte ones are beyond the comprehension of most human beings. The laws of the psychic and spiritual worlds which explain 'miracles' are therefore also the laws of nature. We just need to know the subtle planes on which they operate.

20 February

Adults give very bad advice to young people when they say, 'Go for it, make the most of it, because youth does not last. If you only knew how quickly it passes!' It is true, their youth has passed very quickly, but why? Well, precisely because they listened to this harmful advice when they were young and rushed to enjoy themselves, to experience every pleasure, which is the surest way to lose one's freshness! So, since these are the facts, people draw conclusions. Yes, but if the facts are what they are, it is because they did not know beforehand how to observe and reason correctly.

What I, myself, would say to young boys and young girls is this: if you work for the light, for a high ideal, the older you get, the more alive and expressive you will become. You will even acquire a life and an expression that you did not have when you were younger. Of course, you will stoop a bit, you will have a few more wrinkles and grey hair, but do not let that stop you: allow your body to age gracefully and remember that your soul can continue to manifest through it with an extraordinary youthfulness.

21 February

*M*any men and women have put an end to their life, even if, as we say, 'they had everything they needed to be happy': youth, beauty, intelligence, wealth, family and friends who loved them... They had everything except the most important thing: their taste for life; none of the advantages they had, external or internal, or even the affection of those around them, could give them that.

So it is within themselves that people have work to do, it is inwardly in their soul and in their spirit that they should search for what they need. Only their soul and their spirit will teach them the meaning of life, give them the essence of life, so that no matter what the situation, they will not falter. In the worst situations, they can unite with celestial entities and will feel overjoyed, filled with light. When the cause of your happiness, your fulfillment, is within you, nothing and nobody can deprive you of it. The day you decide to seek the essence within yourself, you will be on the path of freedom, of immortality, of eternity.

22 February

Why are human beings afraid of sacrifice? Why do they reject the idea of sacrifice? Even the word resonates uncomfortably in their ears. Under the pretext that, most often, is to others we must make sacrifices, they think it is others who will gain something at their expense. They feel the sacrifice as a loss and that's why they cut themselves off from the source of life and joy.

A door will suddenly open to those who accept to sacrifice willingly and lovingly, and they will feel overwhelmed by an ocean of light. You don't believe me? But it is nonetheless true. Start by accepting the idea of sacrifice and you will discover that every effort you make for others can strengthen and invigorate you and above all, bring you joy.

23 February

*E*very day we hear people talking about air pollution, every day they complain about fumes from factories, car exhausts. But they themselves, as individuals, what do they often do? Don't they sometimes poison the psychic atmosphere by their toxic emissions: their thoughts and feelings of hatred, jealousy, anger? Be aware that all the unhealthy thoughts, feelings and desires fermenting in human beings produce foul-smelling and suffocating exhalations.

If there were laboratories equipped with sufficiently sophisticated equipment, we would be able to verify that some human emanations are so dirty and impure, that in the psychic world, they have an influence just as toxic as suffocating gas. And we could also come to the opposite conclusion: that the emanations of spiritual beings are extremely beneficial for all creatures. Because such beings have overcome their weaknesses, their presence has a positive effect on all those around them. If the psychic atmosphere of the earth has not yet become completely unbreathable, it is because of the selfless and loving men and women who have dedicated their lives to peace and light.

24 February

Although all human beings are identical in structure, they differ in their sensibility, understanding, needs and aspirations, and as a result they differ in their perception of things. So when they argue with each other about who posseses the truth, what they claim as the truth, is true only to them.

You might say, 'But is there no truth?' On the contrary. The higher we rise within ourselves, the more we detach from our own personal and selfish interests, by purifying ourselves, allowing ourselves to be penetrated by divine light, the closer we come to the truth. But it is impossible to say whether one day we will know the truth in terms of an absolute principle. All we can say with certainty is this: with every effort we make to throw off the opaque layers that have formed around us due to our murky and unrestrained thoughts and sentiments, we come a little closer to the truth.

25 February

*T*o be loved: this is the concept most human beings have of happiness. Of course, they agree to love a little, but they believe that the main thing is to be loved. This is easy to prove: why do they suffer so when they learn that the person they love does not give back that love, or does not give back as much as they wish? They wait for the outside world to give them love. If it does not come, or if it is taken away, they feel deprived: they do not believe in their own power, in their own ability to love, they need love to come from someone outside of themselves.

In reality, to find peace and joy, we must not wait for love to come from other people, but rely only on our own love: because within us lies the source of love, and this source is unlimited.

26 February

One day Jesus reproached his disciples for their disbelief, saying, *'If you have faith the size of a mustard seed, you will say to this mountain, "Move from here to there", and it will move.'* Those who read this verse are so struck by the enormous discrepancy in size of a mountain and a mustard seed that they go no further, and this is why they cannot interpret the parable correctly. Understanding will come from reflecting on the nature and characteristics of a mustard seed.

To have faith no bigger than a mustard seed and to one day be capable of moving mountains... Yes, it is possible because once that seed is sown in our heart and soul, it will grow and expand. And when it becomes a tree, as Jesus said, all the birds of heaven will come and dwell in its branches. The birds of heaven are all the beings of light in the invisible world, and these entities do not come empty-handed. They bring with them heavenly gifts – wisdom, love, purity, peace, and strength – and it is thanks to these gifts that little by little a human being gains the power to move mountains.

27 February

*T*he way in which we consider people and things makes all the difference. If your consciousness is enlightened, each one of your thoughts can be the point of departure for magnificent achievements. If not, you reject the riches which nature and human beings have to offer, and you neither understand, nor gain anything, you feel impoverished and unhappy.

Just look at how human beings live alongside one another: they pass by each other with no more awareness of the other's presence than if they were blocks of stone or pieces of wood. See also how they bump into each other! To talk to them, then, about the relationship they must develop with nature is to expect far too much of them. They believe they are the only beings who are truly alive and intelligent in the universe and, in order to demonstrate this life and this intelligence, what do they do? They exploit nature without any qualms, not realizing that by destroying it, they also destroy something in themselves, they restrict themselves, they become gloomy. It is an entire shift in awareness that must take place within them so that their relations not only with humans but with nature are finally alive and rich.

28 February

*O*ne of woman's vocations is to be the educator of man. By their thoughts, feelings and their attitude, women must inspire men to ever more nobility, righteousness and courage. Men seek only to be uplifted and inspired by women. That is why, until women have this ideal, as long as they think only of satisfying their desires and pleasures or their need for reassurance, they will not fulfil their true vocation, and they themselves will be victims.

You will say, 'But how can women educate men? They are so much weaker and more delicate than men! It is impossible to oppose them?' To influence men, women do not need to oppose them, there are more subtle methods. And women have another means of educating men: by educating her sons. And these sons will respect women all their life thanks to their mother. Yes, through the daily influence they can have over their very young children, mothers are capable of creating upright, noble and generous characters, saints and heroes.

1 March

Seeking to excuse their tactlessness, mistakes, and failures, people will say, 'But I believed this or that...' Ah yes, they believed, they believed... but their believing has only served to lead them astray. And what is worse, these 'believers' will continue to believe and to be led astray. Until when? Until they learn to replace their beliefs by faith, true faith, the faith that is founded on knowledge.

It is clear that we instinctively understand the difference between belief and faith, because we often say, 'I believe', when in fact we are expressing a doubt. If we say, 'I believe he is coming tomorrow,' it means that we are not actually sure. And questions such as, 'Do you believe...?' (for example 'Do you believe that the situation will improve?') show that you are exploring unknown territory. Working in the known, in a domain in which we have extensive experience through sustained effort, this is what it means to have true faith.

2 March

*T*he radio, the telephone, radar, the television and so on are some of the many practical applications of a single discovery: that waves travel through space. But why let science and technology be alone in exploiting this discovery? The waves that allow us to make telephone calls or follow radio or television programmes are not the only ones that travel through space. There are other even subtler waves; the air around us is saturated with currents, with messages we can capture. For the Creator has placed in human beings instruments that allow them to receive waves emitted by the most evolved spirits, the initiates, the angels, the archangels and all the heavenly entities.

So, why stay in communication only with humans, when all you hear from them is shouting, demands, rebelliousness and threats? We must make use of the instruments the Lord has given us (the brain, of course, but also the solar plexus, the hara centre and the chakras), so that we can communicate with beings more evolved than us. When we manage to vibrate on their wavelength we enter into their happiness, their light and their peace.

3 March

*P*eople have sometimes reproached me for the non-scientific and even anti-scientific character of my teaching. Well, they are mistaken, because nothing is more scientific than what I tell you every day, and nothing is more provable, applicable or effective. But this is a different science, and one that surpasses all the others, a science which is the fruit of countless experiments, for I also carry out my experiments in my internal laboratories. You do not believe me? Well, I am not asking that you believe me, but that you also perform these experiments.

Let those who claim to be scientific at least conduct themselves in a scientific manner, which means they should first carry out some experiments and then state their findings. A scientist does not begin with certainties; they state their hypotheses which they then verify through their experiments, allowing whatever time is necessary before presenting the conclusions. So, if you are content to declare you do not believe me without having carried out any experiments, how should we classify you?

4 March

*I*n the realm of politics and economics, when people call for unity, it almost always comprises alliances based on selfish interests, somewhat like those of bandits who unite in order to carry out their attacks? Although this is obviously not unity in the true sense of the word, this is how people think of it – as banding together to pounce on others to expel or even annihilate them. When the citizens of a country say, 'Let's unite!' and the only goal of their union is to attack their neighbour instead of getting along with them, they cannot genuinely speak of unity.

True unity is meant to be all-encompassing. If an organ in the human body establishes unity in itself but fails to work in harmony with the others, it will perhaps feel fine, but the others will suffer, and unity will thus be compromised. When we speak of unity, we are referring to a universal, cosmic unity which excludes nothing and no-one. But this unity must first of all be established within ourselves: all our cells, all our inclinations must be directed towards God. Our efforts to bring this about will be reflected in all other entities, humans and all the little scattered entities will come together to create one universal whole.

5 March

*T*he only way to rightfully resolve relationships with others is to constantly keep in mind the concept of the two natures: lower and higher. Trust only the higher nature, the divine nature, both in yourself and in others.

A human being is like a bank in which you deposit capital. So be vigilant, first make sure that any 'bank' you deal with is solid and reliable, or you will risk losing everything, and there will then be no use in complaining or rebelling. And since you yourself are a bank, strive also to be trustworthy. For it is not merely a question of whether or not you can trust others; ask yourself if they too can trust you, and do your best to deserve this trust. It is this above all that must concern you.

6 March

A man who has made his fortune in business will not always tell you he is happy. Most often, he will find all sorts of reasons to complain. He will tell you that he is stressed, that his wife spends all his money and takes advantage of his absences to cheat on him, that his son is a good-for-nothing and his workers are lazy, that his shares have fallen on the stock exchange, that he will be ruined by his competitors, and so on. You listen to him, and after a while you begin to feel overwhelmed. Despite all his possessions, he could never convince you that life is beautiful, because he lives in fear of losing what he has. So, not only will he give you nothing, since he is already afraid that what he has will be taken away, but he will also rob you of your peace and your love of life.

Whereas a man who has worked to acquire spiritual wealth understands not only that these riches are inexhaustible, but that no one can take them away from him. He will therefore always be ready to share them with you, and thanks to him, whatever your situation, you will be able to to taste the beauty and meaning of life.

7 March

Life is based on the notion of opposites, in other words on the principle of polarity; of active and passive, masculine and feminine, emissive and receptive, good and evil. This opposition is really just a complementarity, and is what creates movement. This concept is expressed in the number 2, which is the number of polarization. 2 is 1 turned into positive and negative.

In Tarot cards, number 2 is represented by the High Priestess, who is holding a book open on her lap. A closed book represents the number 1 and an open book the number 2. People who are able to decipher this arcanum are capable of resolving the problem of evil in their life. They understand that good and evil, love and hate, light and darkness, although opposites in their manifestation, are the two aspects of the same reality. It is pointless, therefore, to want to fight against evil thinking that we will one day destroy it. We must simply learn to use the forces of evil (the problems and the hardships), to transform them into constructive energies.

8 March

*T*hought has an important role to play in our efforts to perfect ourselves. So, those who wish to become wiser, stronger, and more fraternal must set aside time to wish for and visualise these qualities. Imagine yourselves surrounded by light, sending your love across the whole world, and withstanding all difficulties and temptations. Little by little the images you form of these qualities will take on life. They will influence you, they will transform you as they work to attract the necessary elements from the universe and to establish them in your entire being. Of course, a good deal of time and work are necessary before any result is achieved. But the day this result presents itself, you can doubt no longer: you feel a living entity above you which protects you, instructs you, purifies you, enlightens you, and in difficult situations gives you the support you need.

So you should begin by forming some ideal in the world of the spirit. Then, thanks to the thought this perfection will then gradually descend into your psychic matter where it will be realized.

9 March

*I*n whatever you do, think only of spreading beneficial influences. You can do this by means of your hands, which are among the best instruments for transmitting them. When you caress the head of someone you love, instead of seeking egotistical pleasure, concentrate on your hands and say, 'May God bless you. May light reign in this head, and may all angels come and make their home here.' At this moment, your love will no longer be sensual; it will be transformed into a beneficial energy and will also bring you an extraordinary sensation of joy and expansion. And when you touch the head of your child, or its small arms and legs, bless them as well, so that the angels come and make them a magnificent being.

Learn to bless everything you touch: objects, food, and other beings. This is true white magic.

10 March

*I*t is never easy to shake off negative moods. Let us suppose that you are assailed by feelings of animosity, jealousy and bitterness and, however you try to get rid of them, you do not succeed. These are evil entities that cling to you. What should you do? Begin by calmly watching them, how they manifest themselves and their tricks. In doing so, you have already set yourself above them, and this is what happens: sensing the presence of someone watching and studying them, they are uncomfortable, because they do not like being found out. And if, in this moment, you connect to heaven, it is as if you were projecting some rays of light on them; they begin to disperse, because light chases them away.

Obviously these entities will not allow themselves to be dispelled easily, they are stubborn; they can return, of course, and they certainly will; but again you will observe them and project beams of light on them, until at last you manage to get rid of them forever. Yes, because you will have managed to stay above them.

11 March

*S*uppose I walk into a house in the middle of winter where everything is closed, the doors and windows are tightly shut. The air is foul-smelling, because for warmth, the animals have also been allowed in: the cat, the dog, even the horse, and the pig. By staying in this confined atmosphere the inhabitants are completely chloroformed, they feel nothing. If I now have to explain to them that they live in an unhealthy atmosphere, there would be endless discussion, and I would be wasting my time. So I take a different approach and invite them to come out for a walk with me.

We walk in the fresh air for a half hour, or an hour, and then return. When they open the door they exclaim loudly and wonder how they could possibly have existed in this contaminated air – so to speak, since this story is obviously symbolic – with such narrow or erroneous points of view. Without having to explain anything, they themselves understand, because they immediately experience the difference; they make the comparison. Perhaps when they went out they did not fully realize how good it is to breathe fresh air, but on their return when they suffocate, then they understand. And that's what I try to do with you: when I speak to you, I take you for a while into regions where you breathe clean air, so that when you return you decide to leave behind a philosophy that chokes you.

12 March

God is within and without. And the same is true of our higher self; it lives in the sublime regions and also lives within us. But how can we feel the presence of this divine entity which is all-light, all-love and all-powerful? It is difficult, of course, but we must first look within ourselves for signs of that presence, knowing that it is our true self.

It has been said, 'Know thyself.' If a person truly wants to know themself, they have to know themselves up above, in the divine world. Until they are aware of their existence up above as a particle of the Deity, they will not know themselves. To know oneself means to have found oneself by having found God. By finding God, one finds love, light, freedom, joy – and not only does one find these within oneself but also within all human beings and also in animals, plants and stones. When a person finds God within themself, they discover him everywhere, and this is truly to 'Know thyself.'

13 March

*E*ach of us must do what we can to preserve the bonds that unite us to the members of our family. But the family is not an end in itself; it is only a point of departure, a base designed to provide us with a form of stability within society. Those who concentrate on their family and who work for it alone, who forget others or even fight with them in order to better protect their parents or children, do not realize that they are creating the conditions for misunderstanding and hostility, which in the end becomes like a fight between clans, or tribes.

But worst of all, in this state of mind they do not even contribute to the happiness of their own family. As proof, you see that today more and more families are falling apart. After a period of time, parents separate to form ties elsewhere, and the children find themselves with a father on one side, a mother on another, and half-brothers, half-sisters, and so on. So, where is the stability that the family is meant to provide? And is this truly the happiness of family life?

14 March

You will never find the inner stability and security you are looking for as long as you remain in the region of feelings and emotions, in other words in the astral plane*, because here the climate, the atmospheric conditions never stop changing: one moment the sun shines and you are happy, and then along come the clouds and with them sadness. One moment you are in love and then something happens and you are no longer in love. On the astral plane nothing is stable or secure.

We cannot do without feeling, of course not, but do not make the astral plane your home or your shelter. You can go down there, take a walk, look around, study the commotion and the distress that is caused there, but do not live there. Make your home higher up, even beyond the mental plane, because the world of thoughts is not perfectly safe either. How many times do you change your mind or your opinions to suit your own interests? And here again, only disappointment. If you want to be secure you must elevate yourself to the causal plane*. Jesus tells us to build our house on rock. This rock is the symbol of the causal plane.

* See note and diagram, p. 400 and 401.

15 March

When human beings try to resolve their differences by means of force, they can perhaps imagine, for a time, that they have succeeded, but this success will not last. When we impose constraints we always provoke the lower nature in others, the desire to resist, to retaliate, to take revenge. Constraint is felt as violence that always incites hostility, and the result is years and decades of confrontation without ever resolving anything.

The solution is to show kindness, love, and humility. Of course, everything is not resolved right away, because this attitude may at first lead others to believe you are naive and weak, and they may take advantage of this to continue their bad behaviour. But after a while, when they see that your attitude is not dictated by weakness but, on the contrary, by a great spiritual power, they eventually become more open, more conciliatory, and it is then possible for you to get along.

16 March

*T*he annals of Initiatic Science mention that the human species as we know it is not the only one to have appeared on earth. Other species of humans preceded us, some with a far more advanced culture than ours. If they disappeared, it is because they gave free rein to the impulses of their lower nature, which has no other purpose than to control and enslave everything, both human beings and nature.

It is a very bad omen for the future of mankind that we see these tendencies of domination becoming more and more prevalent, especially as scientific and technological advances continue to provide new means. If human beings do not learn to put their lower nature at the service of their higher nature, to the powers of the soul and spirit, then mankind will destroy itself. Cosmic Intelligence, which lives in eternity, can easily spare one more humanity and it will let ours go its own way. So many human species have disappeared already that Cosmic Intelligence would not be troubled if, by its own fault, this humanity also disappeared. With the few remaining individuals, it would prepare a new one.

17 March

*I*n order to receive beneficial currents from space, you have to open up. The Lord has poured out all his blessings in abundance, and if you do not receive them it is because your view of life is so limited that you have severed the bond with him. And then, you complain, 'Oh, nobody hears me, nobody comes to help me, I'm alone, abandoned, it is not possible for God to exist!'

Human beings are extraordinary, they put themselves into deplorable situations, and then they draw the conclusion that God does not exist! No more than that! But if they made some small effort to open themselves to him and communicate with him, they would discover that he has always been there to support and enlighten them, and that if they have not received this help or light, it is because they were closed. Someone who limits themself hurts themself. So make the effort to open up, to expand: you will be captivated with wonder and feel the blessings of the divine presence everywhere – above you, around you and within you.

18 March

We must know how to alternately use the faculties of the intellect and the heart, in other words, to balance the cold current, which circulates in the region of wisdom, with the warm current of love. Truth lies within this balance. If love is not tempered by wisdom, it leads to sentimentality, carelessness, sensuality; but wisdom by itself leads to coldness, contempt and cruelty. Therefore the cold of wisdom must temper the warmth of love, and the warmth of love must moderate the cold of wisdom. Truth – which is life – will find the best conditions in this temperate climate.

If the grain of wheat is to grow normally, it needs just enough warmth and not too much cold either. There is an ideal temperature for all seeds, and why not also for those seeds called human beings? Why would we be an exception?

19 March

*T*o understand suffering and to endure it, do not start to consider it as a heavenly punishment. It is above all a warning, a lesson to stop human beings who are on a slope, from tumbling to their ruin. Yes, when they stubbornly refuse to understand, it is suffering alone that can instruct and save them.

Obviously it would be better not to reach this point, but what else can be done? When Cosmic Intelligence has tried wisdom and explanations by way of the initiates it has sent, when it has tried love and patience by sending saints, prophets and martyrs, and still there is no change, all that is left is to send hardship. It then allows tyrants, criminals and torturers to take over. Cosmic Intelligence only uses suffering as a last resort when, having tried everything, there is no other way to make humans think.

20 March

*F*lowers, trees, oceans, even stones… everything in nature breathes. You might say, 'But I can't imagine the breathing process existing outside of the lungs!' Why not? Life doesn't necessarily need the same organs to ensure the same functions. Look at a tree: it has no lungs, stomach, liver or intestines, and yet it breathes; not only does it breathe, it assimilates, eliminates and reproduces. And it often lives longer than humans! It withstands bad weather; it gives fragrant flowers and fruits. Whereas, with all their abilities, humans are so fragile, the slightest thing can annihilate them.

Most people have the wrong ideas about nature. As far as they are concerned, to be really alive and intelligent means having been created like them. But nature couldn't care less about their opinions and their systems. For nature, it's not necessary to have lungs and a heart to breathe, or a brain to be intelligent. It has created such a multitude of life forms, there will be no end to our discoveries.

21 March

If you want to attract the kindness of heavenly entities so that they further the realisation of your projects, then you must work on harmony.

Wherever they may be, beings of light are attracted by the atmosphere created among those who know how to unite to serve a divine idea. The entities say to each other, 'How different these people are from the countless others who meet only to rant at real or imagined enemies; these beings have decided to work together to prepare the Kingdom of God. We must go to visit them and help them.' Each moment of harmony you manage to create releases a fragrance, a scent that humans may not perceive, but these entities, they smell it. And even the stars up there in the sky, smile at you and send you messages of love.

22 March

*H*ope is not a vague wish for an easier and pleasanter life. It is a wisdom which knows how to use the past and the present in order to project itself into the future and influence it. Hope is the ability to live a magnificent reality that does not yet exist.

So it could be said that hope is a foretaste of a perfect life. Yes, thanks to hope, you eat, drink and nourish yourself with a happiness that you do not yet have, but which is the true reality. For true reality exists not on the physical plane but in the divine world. That you are heirs to heaven and earth is the true reality. Because you are still too young and inexperienced, you cannot yet take possession of your inheritance, but it is there waiting for you. That is what hope is.

23 March

*T*here are so many things to discover when watching the sunrise, so many exercises that enable us to immerse ourselves in this life, this light and this warmth! As the day dawns, a great event is being prepared in the sky. Clouds, sombre or bright, appear and disappear, and all the colours of dawn are like so many signs heralding this one dazzling presence: the sun.

It is worth your while to feel that which signifies the birth of each new day. For billions of years each new day tirelessly recreates the birth of the world's first morning. And how many visible and invisible creatures are also witness to this extraordinary emergence of light! Let us join together to greet the forces of life.

24 March

Men and women who fall in love want their love to never end. This is possible, but only if they understand certain rules and apply them. If you genuinely wish your love for another to last, do not be in a hurry to become physically involved for, once the great passion is over, you will quickly tire of each other and will begin to see each other's failings. To protect your inspiration, try to keep some distance between you.

Those who wish to know and taste everything quickly are soon no longer curious about each other. They do not even want to meet, because they have seen too much and 'eaten' too much; they are saturated, and it is finished. This love which brought them all kinds of blessings, which brought them heaven, has been sacrificed for a few moments of pleasure. Why don't they try to be more vigilant? Why do they deprive themselves so quickly of those subtle, poetic sensations which would have allowed their love to last?

25 March

*T*hose who want to be master of their destiny must not attach so much importance to what comes to them from the outside: difficulties or opportunities, gains or losses. They should just work, knowing that all possibilities are within them, and as a result they will become stronger and increasingly capable of facing all situations – the setbacks as well as the successes, for successes like the setbacks have their dangers.

Whatever realm it may be, you must not trust any outward gain or success. If they come to you, they are welcome, of course, but do not count on them, for nothing outside you is permanent or really belongs to you. Sooner or later it will slip through your hands. You must simply work to strengthen yourself inwardly, to enrich yourself inwardly, in your heart, your mind, your soul and your spirit, so that everything you have acquired is yours forever. And thus you will always feel free and independent.

26 March

'*T*o know, to want, to dare, to be silent.' These four verbs summarize the programme of someone walking on the path of Initiation. 'But why "be silent"?' you might ask. Because from the moment you know what work to do and you have the will to do it and you dare undertake it, there is nothing more to add. The whole of your being will show the results of this work. When you dwell in peace and joy, is it necessary to tell others? No, they see it, they sense it. And if you are living through an inner storm, you may pretend you are swimming in serenity and harmony, no-one will believe you, or they may even laugh in your face. Because here too, everything – the disorder, the noise – shows through.

Human beings tell, explain, and they think that by assembling words and sentences they will manage to convince others. If they really lived what they said, they would not even need to talk. Therefore try to meditate on this really significant precept, 'be silent'.

Some people cannot stand silence because they sense it as a void, an absence: without movement, without life. In fact, there is silence and silence, and in general we can say that there are two kinds: that of death and that of the higher life.

It is this silence of the higher life that we must love and cultivate within ourselves. This silence does not have to do with inertia, but with an intense work that is realized in the midst of perfect harmony. It is neither a void nor an absence, but a fulfilment comparable to the experience of two people united by a great love: they live something so profound that they cannot express it with gestures or words. Yes, true silence is the expression of a presence, the presence of the divine.

28 March

*E*very year in the spring, as the days grow longer and warmer, all the seeds buried in the ground begin to grow. You are well aware of this, you have seen it, but you have not yet understood that the same phenomenon can also take place in you. Indeed, there are seeds in you too, qualities and virtues implanted by God from the very beginning, and if they do not grow, it is because you do not seek to expose yourself to the rays of the spiritual sun.

If, during the first days of spring, we go and watch the sun rise every morning – the sun being the purest image of divinity – it is in order to give our seeds the best conditions in which to grow and manifest. No-one should consider themselves intelligent, learned or sensible enough to scorn this practice, for on the spiritual plane as on the physical plane, seeds need the sun to grow.

29 March

*O*bjective reality does not really exist: for every human being, the only reality is what they live and feel. Take the case of someone who has hallucinations: they feel that they are pursued by monsters, they are terrified and flee screaming. Physically, visibly, no one is attacking them, but they feel persecuted, and are suffering, and when someone suffers, try telling them that it is only an illusion! Their suffering is real! In the same way, in the middle of the worst material situations, certain human beings can experience illumination and ecstasy. Once again, how can they be persuaded that it is not real? They are truly immersed in joy.

The suffering and joy we feel are perhaps the only things we never doubt. In effect, we can doubt what we see, what we hear, and what we touch, but what we feel, what we live, can never be doubted; this is reality. In this sense, it can be said that the human being is the master of reality, because if they decide to bring heaven to life within themselves, they will achieve it, and whatever the conditions, it is heaven that they will experience.

30 March

*A*nimosity and hatred arise between human beings because face-to-face with one another they are never conscious that they are in the presence of a spirit, a spark that is seeking to manifest itself and that, in order to help this spirit before them, it is worth their while to be kind, patient, understanding and generous. Given the way they are used to seeing each other and what they see in each other when they meet, it is inevitable that they end up wanting to kill each other.

And even Christians who have, supposedly, placed the love of one's neighbour as the foundation of their religion, do they not continue to live in hostility and confrontation? Yes. And why? Precisely because they never see beyond people's lower nature. If they understood that there was a spirit and a soul in them to which they could relate, they would feel obliged to behave differently.

31 March

*E*ach thing, each being in creation has two poles. Take for example a tree: it feeds on air and light through its branches and leaves while it feeds on water and earth through its roots. Just like the tree, man receives forces from above and forces from below.

When Adam and Eve lived in paradise in the Garden of Eden, it was as if they lived amongst flowers. Flowers are exposed to the air, to the light of the sun and are visited by butterflies and bees. In the flowers one lives a heavenly and radiant life. But the day Adam and Eve, under the influence of the serpent, left the flowers and went down through the trunk to the roots of the cosmic tree, they had to endure darkness and cold; they thus felt the weight of matter, and everything – moving, eating, etc – became more difficult. Human beings are in the same situation today. But the work of the disciple is precisely to learn to control and use the subterranean forces they draw from their roots so as to produce flowers and bear fruit at the summit of their being.

1 April

*T*here are so many people in the world with whom you think you would have better conditions to work and grow. Why is it that in your family, at work or elsewhere, you are surrounded by particular people, and not others? Instead of complaining, reacting, or losing courage, you should reflect and question yourself.True, some situations seem at first glance unexplainable, unbearable; but even if you do not understand, make the effort to think they have a meaning, a purpose. And the more incomprehensible and contrary it is to what you would hope for, the more you have to trust heaven and tell yourself that this is the way to your most cherished aspirations. Even if for the moment you are struggling, after some time you will strengthen yourself, your relationships with others will improve, and you will feel good influences even on your health.

2 *April*

*T*he legendary knight Perceval, or Parsifal, who sets out in quest of the Holy Grail, has become in the initiatic tradition the image of the adept on the path of initiation. Like Parsifal, who must cross dark forests, fight formidable enemies, and elude snares, the disciple meets with darkness, temptations, dangers and enemies in their personal life.

Once all these obstacles are overcome, Parsifal comes to a marvellous castle whose walls are decorated with gold and precious stones, where he is welcomed impressively; and it is here that he is allowed to contemplate the Holy Grail, the sacred vessel. The sight of the Grail symbolizes the supreme reward for the person who makes their inner being a palace where the walls are covered with gold and precious stones. For they never cease to nourish within them the highest ideal: to acquire the inestimable gifts of the spirit.

3 April

You believe that God does not protect you, that he has allowed evil and the wicked to triumph over you. You go about settling your accounts with him, and in your consciousness you begin to distance yourself from him. But you must understand that to settle your accounts with God leads to nowhere except more losses of something very precious. So, if this happens to you, you must now turn back, and say, 'Lord, I thought I could get away from you, that I could get by without you, but now I am doubly unhappy. Forgive me.'

Until you have understood that nothing can separate you from God, you will only add spiritual misery to your moral and physical suffering. Yes, by cutting yourself off from the source of life, light and love, you are depriving yourself of that which sustains, nourishes and inspires you. Never forget that this source also flows within you, and that it is this which nourishes your soul and your spirit.

4 April

Sooner or later there comes a time when human beings take stock of their lives. And then, if they are honest they are often obliged to recognize that they have wasted their energy, their health and their beauty on somewhat worthless activities. Of course, they have derived a few advantages from them, but if they put them all on the divine scales, they see that the little they have gained does not compensate for the wealth they have lost.

Unfortunately, men and women often make this type of assessment much too late. When they set out on their conquest of money, glory or knowledge, it does not occur to them to assess the losses these pursuits could entail. And even if they are proud to have achieved their goal, a few years later we find them exhausted, physically and mentally ill, having lost their appetite, sleep and joy. Then they realize that what they earned did not justify all this trouble, and they say, 'If only I had known!' But it is too late; they should have made this assessment much earlier!

5 April

*E*ach of our psychic states produces an effect in the invisible world, and will therefore affect other creatures. Even if most human beings are not aware of this, it does not change anything; sooner or later they will be obliged to take note of all the damage caused by their internal disorders. When they arrive in the other world the heavenly beings will say, 'Look, it is your fault that this crime was committed, that this accident happened.' They may well protest that they never did anything wrong, that they never stole, or destroyed anything, or killed anyone. But the response will be, 'Perhaps not, but your bad thoughts and feelings created negative currents that influenced others, and because of you, they were pushed to do wrong.'

Before divine Justice we are not only responsible for our actions. Each of us is equally responsible for their thoughts, feelings, and desires, because they act in the invisible world as forces capable of leading other beings towards good or evil.

6 April

You are looking at a balloon on a string. It strains to rise into the sky, but it is tied to the ground. Like this balloon, all human beings have something within them which aspires to escape, to rise freely into the air, but which is restrained by its bonds. Well these bonds, we must try bit by bit to loosen or untie them, to allow this eternal aspiration, which is engraved in our soul, this yearning to fly to the immensity of light and peace from whence we came.

It is from this memory, often vague and confused, of a distant and lost homeland – a memory often vague and confused – from which most humans draw their faith, for they bear it unconsciously within them, an indelible trace of a far distant past when they dwelt in the bosom of the Eternal, and they retain this nostalgia.

7 April

Roots, a trunk, and branches are not sufficient: a tree is only truly a tree when – having been worked on by the universal spirit – it begins to produce leaves, flowers, and fruits. It is the same for human beings. We possess a stomach, lungs, and a brain, but is this sufficient to call ourselves fully developed beings? No, like the roots, trunk, and branches, of a tree, our organs are only a material support upon which the spirit must work in order to bear leaves, flowers, and fruits. Symbolically, the leaves represent the activity of the stomach, flowers that of the lungs, and fruits that of the brain.

The descent of the spirit into a human being is comparable to the arrival of spring, which allows the tree to manifest all the riches it bears within it.

8 April

Why is God presented as someone who watches human beings day and night and writes in a little notebook all the faults they are openly or secretly committing? In fact, the Lord is not concerned with the faults of human beings. Let's say he spends his time at banquets partaking of nectar and ambrosia, and all the angels rejoice with him singing and their musical instruments.

So, you will ask, what happens when we make mistakes? It is very simple. If human beings had the idea to create recording machines, it is because such machines already exist in nature, and thus in themselves as well. And these 'machines' record their thoughts, feelings, and actions. When they transgress certain limits, in whatever realm it may be, a mechanism is set in motion and they lose something, either on the physical, the emotional, or the mental plane. This is our punishment; it is not God who punishes us. On the contrary, God is always ready to receive us at heaven's banquets.

9 April

*F*or most human beings, to love means to ask, to demand, to require. Yes, literally! This is how people conduct themselves with the Lord, and also with those they claim to love: they pursue them with their demands and, no matter what they receive, they are never satisfied.

So you want some criteria for knowing whether you really love a human being? If you ask nothing of them, if your only desire is to thank them and thank heaven only because this human being is there, because they exist, yes, just because they exist, you can be sure that you love. Otherwise, give your feelings whatever name you want, whatever they are, they are not love.

10 April

You long for freedom? Whatever happens to you, do not become troubled or discouraged, but see to it that your spirit gradually regains control of the situation. Because only the spirit is truly free and soars high over events.

When you restore the spirit to its place within you, something tells you that no obstacle, no hardship, can destroy your balance, your peace or your love, on the contrary. And since these illuminating experiences have taught you values you can count on, cling to them. Do not doubt the beautiful and great things you have lived, but take them along with you as provisions on this difficult path you must travel. When the storm has passed, you will realize that these trials which might have caused you to lose heart, have actually strengthened you.

11 April

*B*ecause the consequences of their thinking and behaviour are not immediate, human beings rarely notice what has caused their misfortune. When they succumb to inner disorder or behave disgracefully, it is rare that a catastrophe befalls them at once; they feel no different, and sometimes they even feel better than before. Why has Cosmic Intelligence arranged things in this way? In order to give human beings the time and the opportunity to become aware of their errors and to correct them. Instead of allowing the law of cause and effect to come into play immediately, Cosmic Intelligence in its wisdom and love grants us credit; it gives us time to reflect and rectify our behaviour.

Someone transgresses certain rules of society, for example, you do not declare your correct income in your tax return, the tax office will ask for your accounts a few months or a few years later. And while awaiting its decision, you will still have time to rectify the situation. The same thing applies to the inner life: this opportunity given to human beings to make amends, to correct themselves, is an aspect of divine wisdom and divine love.

12 April

We are on earth for a reason, or the Lords of Destiny would have sent us elsewhere. There are plenty of places in the universe for a pleasant vacation.

The best place to go, in fact, is the sun. You will say, 'The sun? But we will be burned!' Yes, of course, if you go there in your physical body, but who said that you must do that? The physical body is adapted to life on earth. In order to go to other planets or to the sun, you have other bodies, other vehicles. There are different forms of life in the universe which correspond to different aspects of matter and, although we cannot go to the sun in our physical body, we can at least go there with our soul and our spirit.

13 April

*T*he host that Christians receive at communion is intended to remind them of the bread given to his disciples at the Last Supper by Jesus saying, *'Take, eat; this is my body.'* Since it contains more or less the same ingredients as bread, in the material sense the host offers nothing more than a little mouthful of bread. But it has been given a symbolic function: it represents the body of Christ. Through his blessing, the priest communicates spiritual energies to this host, and it is up to the believer who receives it to understand its sacred significance.

So ultimately, is it not the believer who has the most important role? By their inner attitude, they can diminish the blessing the priest has given it, or, on the contrary, they can reinforce it, depending on the respect, the consideration they give the host.

14 April

*A*ll the beings and things round us may help us, but we must never count on them absolutely. Since they are exterior to us, they may not always be available; one moment they are there, and the next they are elsewhere, or someone may even come and take them from us.

The true disciple of Initiatic Science learns that they must look inside themself for what they need to live in plenitude. Because it is in their soul and spirit that God has deposited all riches. And since the riches are within them, they remain theirs. Of course, the exploration of this inner world is a long-term undertaking that demands daily effort, but nothing else can truly fulfil the disciple. The nourishment we obtain from the sublime realms of the soul and spirit satisfies us for days and days. And nothing or nobody can take away this sensation of space and eternity.

15 April

A religion is a form through which the divine spirit manifests, and no form is permanent. Christianity, which was born in the Middle East, received at its inception certain elements from the Greek and Latin cultures. To these were added elements inherited from the Jewish religion, which itself had been influenced by the religions of neighbouring countries such as Egypt and Mesopotamia. A religion is never born from nothing; it takes on elements from previous religions and is itself transformed as it spreads far from its place of origin. The peoples of Africa, America and Asia who have been converted to Christianity, for example, have added elements from their own cultures.

Whether we like it or not, religions change. Even if they are the same sacred texts, an ever-widening gap exists between what people read and how they understand and feel about them. Evolution is the law of life, which is why it is illogical to strive to perpetuate the forms of a religion.

16 April

Nothing in the world has a value greater than, or even equal to life, and our first duty is to preserve our life, to protect it, to make it more powerful, more intense. History has told of men and women who gave their lives standing up for certain ideas, to save victims, people in danger. Saints, prophets, initiates have also given their lives for an idea, for the glory of God; not only did they not lose anything, but thereafter received a new life, even richer and more beautiful, because they had sacrificed themselves for the good. But apart from these cases, which are the exception, each person must conserve their life, preserve it, purify, intensify and enlighten it, for life is the source, the point of departure of all other developments on the physical, emotional and mental planes.

True resurrection begins by working on life. At the beginning, there is life, then come wisdom, love, beauty, etc., as many branches of the primordial tree of life.

17 April

The spiritual evolution of a human being is accompanied by an increase in their sensitivity. The more our sensitivity increases the more abundant and intense our life becomes. If our sensitivity decreases we return to the animal, vegetable and mineral kingdoms. You mightl say, 'But the greater our sensitivity, the greater the chance of us suffering.' That is true, but even if one risks becoming more vulnerable, it is preferable, because with increased sensitivity comes a greater intensity of life.

As for the people who have great sensitivity, take care to preserve it by knowing moderation. For it is excess that dulls sensitivity. If you read too much, for instance, your brain becomes saturated and you no longer enjoy thinking. If you want to understand the essential points, you must avoid accumulating too many ideas in your head. And this goes for friendship and love too. You must watch yourself, keep a certain distance, because if you throw yourself headlong into the thrills of love you will soon become bored and feel nothing. Sensitivity develops in people who know how to reduce the quantity and increase the quality.

18 April

*E*ach of us possesses a soul, and this soul has needs. If so many human beings are unconscious of these needs, it is because they have stifled them by leading a life without ideals. But these needs are there, and sometimes they manifest in people but they do not understand the language. All these dangerous experiments – like drugs for example – that today tempt young people as well as adults, are expressions of something they are lacking, a call of the soul, hungry for the infinite, and demanding to be nourished.

Indeed, what is left for the soul in a society which flouts all belief in a divine world, and in which political rivalries and economic and social success are held up as ideals? Since we deprive the soul of the spiritual foods it needs to be able to soar into space, it looks for these elements in the material realm, in substances such as tobacco, alcohol and drugs, all that we call 'artificial paradises'. But then these substances destroy humans physically and psychically.

19 April

A true spiritualist is one who decides to abandon all their futile occupations, all their passing pleasures that bring them nothing. By doing this, they release within themselves spiritual energies that were paralysed and enslaved by ordinary, everyday habits, and they can at last bear fruit in the land of the soul and the spirit.

Look at a tree: when it is invaded by insects and caterpillars, it cannot bear fruit, and we must rid it of its parasites. In the same way, someone who indulges in laziness, a life of ease and frivolous distractions attracts parasites. And what are these parasites? Dark entities of the astral world. They invade their body, will, heart and intellect, they suck up the sap that should nourish their higher self. Yes, this is true: if they are not vigilant, human beings become the home of other beings that drain them of all their energy. To get rid of these parasites, they must dedicate their whole being to their higher self, thereby nourishing it with succulent fruits.

20 April

We cannot live without making exchanges with the world around us. Beginning with respiration and nutrition, our life is nothing more than exchanges, made possible by our sense organs (touch, taste, smell, hearing and sight), which have been given to us by nature to allow exchanges with creation and its creatures. Our emotional and intellectual lives also consist of encounters and exchanges: by means of words, feelings and thoughts, we ceaselessly weave a network of relationships which is the foundation of family and social life.

If human beings do not derive any great benefits from these exchanges, it is often because they do not rise above the level of instinct, of the unconscious as it exists in plants and animals. Like human beings, plants and animals breathe and nourish themselves. Animals also possess sense organs, sometimes even more highly developed than those of human beings, and they also have a family and social life. It is the responsibility of humans to make all their exchanges with nature and the other beings they encounter, more profound and richer. And our teaching provides many exercises for doing this.

21 April

*E*ducating a child does not only mean lecturing, giving orders, and punishment when they disobey. To become good educators, adults must think about the qualities and virtues that dwell within the soul and spirit of the child and then focus on the divine spark living within, to give this spark all the conditions it needs to express itself. In this way they would foster the growth of these magnificent seeds within the child later on.

And because a child does not always understand what is being said, or why, you should also address their subconscious. For example when they are asleep, the parent or carer can go beside the child's bed, and without waking them, caress them lightly, speak to them about all the good they wish them. In this way, they place deep in the child's being, precious elements that, when revealed years later, will protect them from many mistakes and dangers.

22 *April*

*E*very day you are confronted with the manifestations of your lower nature. It is part of you, it presents its arguments to you. But beware, and try not to allow yourself to be convinced, never give it this right. If you wish, grant your lower nature the benefit of being 'unreasonably correct' by saying, 'Alright, for reasons which were undoubtedly valid in the past, at a certain stage of evolution when for their survival, human beings, like animals, had to obey their instincts. But now, at a more advanced stage of evolution, Cosmic Intelligence has other plans for me.'

And do not trust those who allow themselves to be directed by their lower nature. You can excuse them by understanding the cause of their behaviour, but do not be influenced by them. To understand them, to excuse them and forgive them is something different; and with some exceptions, can even be advisable. But as for you, follow your higher nature; in doing so, you will always be on the right path and by following this path you can also show others the way.

23 April

When human beings attack and destroy one another, they are working against the Creator. Even if God has created them different, these differences must never serve as a pretext for fighting one another. In the eyes of God, nothing justifies hatred for a certain race or people, or the desire to enslave a social class. All living beings were born of God, and he suffers as a result of their clashes.

Human beings have adopted a philosophy of separateness in the name of interests they claim to be superior, but which in fact are only inspired by their selfishness and shortsightedness. The defence of these interests goes against the interests of all creation, and it will be their downfall. The true interests of humanity and those of the Divinity are one and the same, and only when they unite will blessings come to pass for all.

24 April

*E*ven if they have a good imagination, the majority of human beings do not know what this faculty really is. True imagination, such as the initiates conceive it and with which they work, is a type of screen located at the boundary between the visible and invisible worlds. On this screen are reflected objects and entities that normally escape our consciousness. In some very evolved beings that know how to direct their imagination, this screen receives and records many things that they then express and manifest. Later, we perceive that what they had thus 'imagined' was not pure invention on their part, but that they had captured realities which had not yet appeared on the physical plane.

All humans possess this ability to capture the realities of the invisible world, but only those who know how to work on their thoughts and feelings succeed in purifying their mental body to such a degree that their imagination becomes clear – pure and transparent – and they begin to 'see'. At this level, imagination and vision are one.

25 April

Never give away your heart; it belongs to you and no-one has the right to do what they want with it. If you give your heart to someone, you no longer have it. The other person has two hearts, but what will they do with two hearts? They will end up letting go of yours. There is a saying in Bulgaria that you can't carry two watermelons under one arm. So some time or another the person to whom you have given your heart could drop it. And then you will cry out, 'My heart is broken!' And if you go to complain to Heaven, it will say, 'it is your fault; why did you give it away? You should have kept it for yourself.' 'Yes but I love them, I love them.' Alright, so you love them, but you could have given them your tenderness, your love, your songs, and kept your heart for yourself.

And do not be misled into thinking that this warning applies only to the heart. Nature has also given us a body, a mind, a will, and those who are wise will keep these for themselves. They will give away only the fruits, in other words thoughts, feelings, activity and work.

26 April

It is said in the *Zend-Avesta* that when Zoroaster asked the god Ahura-Mazda how primordial man fed themselves, he answered that they ate fire and drank light. Why do we not also learn to eat fire and drink light, to return to the perfection of primordial man? You will say it is not possible. Yes it is possible.

You are watching the sun rise; wait, watchful and attentive. As soon as the first ray appears, concentrate on absorbing it. So instead of simply watching the sunrise, you are drinking it, you are eating it, and you imagine that this living light spreads through all the cells of your organs, purifying them, strengthening them and enlivening them. This exercise not only helps you concentrate, but you will feel your entire being start to quiver and illuminate because you are truly absorbing light.

27 April

Sight, hearing, smell, taste and touch give us a good knowledge of material reality. But the five senses have extensions into the psychic world, and for those who have learned to use them they are also helpful in their relationships with others. The eyes allow us to interpret imperceptible details of behavior. The ear can analyze, even beyond spoken words, the intonations of a voice, even on the telephone. Smell detects the odour of psychic emanations and taste allows us to distinguish their flavour. And with touch, when we shake hands, we are immediately informed of a person's character, for in a handshake our whole being is expressed.

So many people regret not seeing more clearly when meeting others! They have overestimated some, underestimated others. Why? Because they are always too quick to pass judgment. It is based on a first impression, and often to suit themselves. From now on, you must be in less of a hurry, more careful and attentive, for you know that, although it is difficult to know human beings, the five senses, used effectively, can already give us some indications.

28 April

*T*hose who do not rebel against their difficulties and hardships, but accept to understand and learn from them liberate the powers in their soul and spirit. After a time they realize that something magnificent has occurred within them as a result. Many people say they feel attracted to alchemy! Well this is the true work of alchemy. When you understand this you will be able to extract from the raw, black, formless matter of suffering, a matter that is precious, sparkling, iridescent and dazzling with a thousand colours.

Since suffering is inevitable you should learn to work with it, otherwise you will resemble abandoned construction sites: when you wish to express yourself, you will not know what materials to use. You will know nothing of the life of the soul and spirit – of its immensity, its depths and its heights. Only those who know how to suffer can become creators.

29 April

*F*or most people, the slightest annoyance sets off an entire mechanism within them. They take any opportunity to mull over their thoughts and feelings of irritation, anger, resentment and revolt. They judge everything others do in terms of their own desires and expectations, and let others beware if they do not meet these expectations! Not only do they hold grudges against others, but they attribute all kinds of malevolent intentions to them. They do not ask themselves whether these people are busy or otherwise occupied, whether they have problems or are ill, and whether their behaviour could possibly be justified by their current situation. Why should they ask themselves such questions? They prefer to interpret their behaviour as personal affronts.

Human beings will be much better off when they realize that it is not others who inflict the most harm, but they themselves, because they continually listen to their lower nature. It is this lower nature, so neurotic, which at every opportunity, feeds on false ideas and mistaken beliefs that they should be wary of.

30 April

*H*ave you seen a classroom before the teacher arrives? The children are all running around, shouting and squabbling among themselves. This is normal, because 'when the cat is away, the mice will play.' But look what happens when the teacher comes in: within seconds, all the children sit down because the head, the leader has arrived. Well, these same laws exist within us. God is the head, the leader, the centre, but on condition we allow him in, otherwise chaos will reign within us.

When I hear someone say, 'I have no need for God, I can get along without him,' I agree that he can get along very well without him, but in what disorder, what darkness and at what cost! The head, God, establishes order among the cells of our organism. When He is present they work in perfect harmony, and life circulates. It is essential to have God as the centre within you because it is this point, at the centre, which organizes and harmonizes our entire inner being.

1 May

*Y*ou wish, for example, to wear a talisman to shelter you from the aggression of the psychic world, so you go into a shop where you buy a pentagram, the five-pointed star, because you have read that this symbol has special protective properties. Well, think again: wearing this pentagram or placing it at the entrance of your home, will not protect you if you do not yourself, by your inner work, impregnate it with pure and harmonious vibrations. And even if a great mage may have prepared it for you, this talisman cannot continue to be effective and powerful if you do not work to acquire the virtues symbolized by the pentagram: love, wisdom, truth, justice, kindness.

The pentagram is, in a way, like the skeleton of a spirit on the astral plane, but it has to be given life in order to stand guard near you or at the entrance of your home and to protect you from evil entities. And you can only energise it by your own life, a life of honesty, integrity in the service of light.

2 May

Ask people about their likings and you will discover an extraordinary diversity. Everyone has likes and dislikes which vary according to their temperament. Whether it comes from the head, heart, stomach, genitals, there is always something within us that wants to lead us in a certain direction. But this is not a reason to follow it blindly; before giving in to an impulse, we must ask ourselves what the consequences will be.

Those whose consciousness is not awakened can find pleasure in pursuits that are pointless and even harmful for their evolution. Whatever their appetites, they seek to satisfy them. But they should not be surprised if these joys quickly turn into suffering, bitterness, and regret. Only the pleasures of a wise and enlightened being remain pure gold. You should not deprive yourself of joys or pleasures, you should just be aware of their nature and always try to replace them with joys and pleasures that are purer, nobler and more beneficial for yourself and for others.

3 May

What is the relationship between the serpent and the dove? They represent the two opposing aspects of the same energy – sexual energy. The dove is none other than the serpent sublimated. It teaches us that anything that crawls on the earth may one day be able to take to the air and fly.

The serpent represents primitive sexual power, and it is very wily! As is written in Genesis, *'Now the serpent was more crafty than any other wild animal that the Lord God had made.'* It is impossible to count all the possible means that humans use to escape the serpent, but it presents and arranges things in such a way that, more often than not, it ends up gaining the upper hand. Someone will say, 'There! I won't succumb to temptation, I'll resist...' But, having failed to foresee the trap the serpent is able to prepare, at the moment they least expect it, they fall into it. And they will keep doing so until they succeed in transforming the serpent within into a dove, that is to say, in transforming human love into spiritual love, which will lift them away from the earth and allow them to know the freedom of infinite space.

4 May

We meet people who claim to be atheists, and yet they say they envy those who have faith. But this is as far as they go. They behave as if having or not having faith has absolutely nothing to do with them, as if faith were a gift we either receive or do not receive from nature. And this is where they are mistaken, faith is in fact the crystallisation of past knowledge; a past experience from the divine world, an experience which has left indelible traces within each of us which we must bring to life.

It is when people are confused by the sense of these traces within them, that they regret their lack of faith; they understand that something essential is missing. But if they do nothing to rediscover their faith, they will suffer this lack even longer, and with increasing intensity. Faith is the result of work. So we should not think that by doing nothing, we can find faith just like that, suddenly, as a result of an unexpected divine grace. It is impossible; even to acquire faith and to maintain it, you have to work.

5 May

*T*he more of us there are when we come together, the more our fraternal radiance attracts divine entities that come to help, giving us health, strength, and light. We do not gather together because we are happy to see each other and to pass the time in a pleasant way, but to do conscious work. And this work consists of submitting our personal, limited life to the law of brotherhood, universality, and harmony. Each harmonious vibration we create attunes us to the great cosmic harmony.

The word 'harmony' embodies every virtue, all blessings. When harmony penetrates every region of our being, it will tune us like an instrument; the Spirit will then touch us with its breath and draw out the most beautiful sounds. This is what it means to work for the kingdom of God.

6 May

*I*t is not so much on the physical plane that we must try to sort things out, for the physical plane is the world of consequences, over which we have very little power. In order to bring about lasting change, we must rise, through thought, to the world of causes, for it is only there that we have all the means to contact and trigger beneficial forces that will sooner or later produce some results. But most people ignore this. They content themselves with intervening on the physical plane. And then they are surprised to see that the improvements they have managed to achieve do not last; events or people come and arrange things their own way without consulting them. And so they are never in control of the situation.

The same law applies to an individual. If you want, for example, to change your bad habits, do not tackle them directly. Try to rise, through thought, to the causal plane*, for it is up there, by uniting with the world of wisdom, love and truth, that you will be able to release powers, which will have an influence on your behaviour.

* See note and diagram, p. 400 and 401.

7 May

*I*n the sacred books it is said that the souls of the virtuous exhale scents that are the delight of the Lord and celestial entities. And it is true: the soul of a virtuous person gives off a scent, and that scent attracts the angels, it attracts the Holy Spirit. The Holy Spirit descends only into a soul in which it can inhale the scent.

It is therefore very important for us to manage, through our spiritual work, to improve the quality of our scent, that is to say, our psychic emanations, not so much to attract humans, but to attract friends from the invisible world. Why not offer them this joy? You say you burn incense... It's good, but it is not enough; if you want to attract the angels, it is also within that you must learn to exhale the fragrance of purity and holiness.

8 May

*T*o discover the presence of God within us, the best exercise is to seek to identify with him. But to identify with the Lord does not mean imagining that we have succeeded in reaching him, and from there, on high, declaring ourselves omniscient and all-powerful. Those who practise this exercise of identification must desire only to be permeated by the immensity of God, to diminish and melt into his vastness.

In relation to other human beings, we often have to assert ourselves, to resist, to oppose even, so that we do not disappear. But before God, when we diminish ourself, by being humble before him, we strengthen ourselves and grow. The law of polarisation also operates in this realm: the great and the small attract each other. God, who is infinitely great, loves the infinitely small, so if you become small, God draws you to him. It is humility which will enable you to become truly one with him.

9 May

*E*ven if human beings complain how rushed and feverish their lives are, they accept their way of life. For some, all this constant tension and stress is what true life is all about. They rush from one place to another, meeting briefly with countless people, spend hours on the phone, doing deals everywhere, and this is their idea of being active and creative. It is in silence, however, that true activity is generated. It is in silence that the greatest achievements are attained, where immortal creations are made.

From time to time, think of stopping for a while; try to feel the intense life that pulsates at the heart of this absence of noise and apparent stillness. Silence is where you will find fulfilment and perfect movement. Once you become conscious of this you will find within yourself the type of silence from which will spring your most beautiful spiritual creations.

10 May

Love between human beings can often be compared to an old wood stove whose smoke is constantly blackening their inner being. In winter when this stove is in use, they keep the windows closed, there's no air, they then doze off and lose their vitality. But then with spring, the sun of spiritual love arrives, and they open the windows very wide, pure air comes in and then they revive!

What lessons should we draw from these images? That we should keep some distance from this old wood stove – that is, from our instincts, from our lusts – for they keep the windows of our soul closed, they prevent air from coming in, they oppose what is most alive within us. And do not fear that a life modelled on moderation and reason will bore you to death. When you feel the gentle touch of divine wisdom and love, you will see for yourself that these passionate experiences that were so important to you before, will be no more than a little ash. Your inner home will become luminous and pure, and you will experience true joy.

11 May

*S*ome psychologists justify the disobedience and insolence of children and adolescents claiming that because young people are much more intelligent and gifted than their parents, it is normal that they should stand up to them. It is true that there are gifted children but they are very rare, and it is not true that most children are geniuses and have a right to rebel against their mediocre parents. No.

You must understand first of all that there is a reason why a child is born into a particular family, because nothing happens by chance. The lords of destiny act with wisdom and justice, and once the child has arrived it is too late to challenge the situation. If they incarnated into this family they were either born there because they deserved it, or to carry out a special apprenticeship, and this apprenticeship consists first of all in accepting their parents. Later on, who can say, but in becoming a member of this family, they first have to do their best to live in harmony with them. When they have proved their true superiority they can do as they wish, but not before.

12 May

Wherever we go and whatever beings or objects we touch, we leave traces. We say of those who are evil that where they have walked, grass will not grow. And symbolically at least, this is no exaggeration. Others, on the contrary, who think only to enlighten, invigorate, comfort and liberate others, leave such life-giving and luminous imprints wherever they go, that those who come after them suddenly feel regenerated.

So, wherever you are, remember to offer your best wishes: 'May all those who come here be touched by the love and brotherhood. Let them discover the true life. May they become children of God and work for the coming of his kingdom on earth!' Everywhere, whether you are in the city or the country, whether you are walking down a street or a path, bless this street or this path with your thoughts. Ask that all those who pass this way may receive life, peace, light and hope.

13 May

*H*uman beings have a natural tendency to meet their needs and solve their problems without taking others into account, and even if it suits them, at the expense of others. Well, these are serious mistakes. For your own benefit, I will tell you that you must now decide not to work for yourself alone, but for the collective whole. Yes, it is in your own interest because you are a part of this community.

When the community improves and evolves, you benefit from these improvements. You reap the benefit because you have placed your capital in a bank called the human family or the universal brotherhood, of which you are a member. Whereas when you work for the sole benefit of yourself, nothing good happens to you. You will say, 'But I disagree, I have been working for myself.' No, because your separate and egotistic self is a bottomless pit which is always dissatisfied and, by working for it, you throw everything into it. You must therefore change the purpose of your work and place it very high in an ideal of universality.

14 May

*T*he intellect is a faculty which allows people to know the physical world and a little of the psychic world, but nothing more. It is thus a very limited faculty. The intellect alone cannot know the truth. The truth of a rose cannot be described and analysed merely in terms of its form, its colour and its perfume. The truth of a rose is its soul and its emanation, an entire collection of elements which make it a rose and nothing else.

And the same thing applies to human beings. The truth about them is much more than we see; it encompasses everything about them: their feelings, their thoughts, their actions, their soul, their spirit. Until we know these, we do not know the truth about them; we have only a few notions about their appearance and their behaviour. Truth about the human being is a synthesis which can be known only by the faculty we call intuition.

15 May

The metamorphosis of a caterpillar into a butterfly is a process that has its equivalent in our psychic life. For a period of their existence (and this period could last for centuries), a human being is like a caterpillar who needs to eat leaves. That is to say, they satisfy their appetites at the expense of others whom they contaminate and shred. But one day they become ashamed of their behaviour and decide to improve themselves. Then they start to go within and they pray, they meditate, and create a cocoon to protect their inner work. Until one day a butterfly emerges from this cocoon and flies through the air.

You will ask, 'What is this cocoon we have to prepare?' It is the aura. A disciple who understands the power of the aura and who works on it no longer 'eats' people, just as the butterfly no longer eats leaves, but flies lightly from flower to flower and feeds on their nectar. The difference between an ordinary man and an initiate can be summarised in a few words: how you feed yourself.

16 May

*T*he tongue is a precious tool; but it was not given to man to be used, as it unfortunately is much of the time, to weaken or destroy others. Its true vocation is to help those who have fallen, to enlighten, encourage and to guide those who search for their path. If in this life, some people are deprived of the ability to speak, it could be that this disability has been given to them as a punishment for the wrong they have done in a past life, by cursing, slandering or wrongly accusing people. The tongue was given to man only to bless, give thanks and communicate with wisdom, justice and love. One day, those who do not know the value of this treasure they possess will lose it in one way or another.

The tongue is responsible for many events in our lives, both happy and unhappy; it is our tongue that makes us lose or win friends. So try to show that you are wise, good and honest, and can control you tongue by always finding a kind word for others.

17 May

In the book of *Genesis*, it is said that Adam and Eve, having disobeyed God were driven out of Paradise. But this is only a symbolic story of the descent of human beings into matter. This descent, in fact, was neither a mistake nor an accident; it was foreseen by Cosmic Intelligence. Why? Because in order to attain a more complete knowledge, human beings were required to develop their intellectual faculties. To develop these faculties, they had to devote themselves to the exploration of matter, which meant placing themselves in conditions which temporarily diminished their perception of the spiritual world.

Human beings today find themselves at a stage of their development where they are immersed in materialism. But it is not the final stage: when this experience is complete, they will return to the regions of the soul and spirit which they have left, and thanks to all they have experienced in the material realm by way of the intellect, they will return enriched.

18 May

*O*ur higher self, our divine self is constantly sending us messages; and if we do not receive them, or if we receive them wrongly, it is because we have accumulated too many impurities within us. Consider an oil lamp whose glass is smoky: its flame is not as luminous, as far-reaching or as beautiful as when the glass is absolutely transparent; it must be cleaned.

A human being can be likened to an oil lamp: their inner light wants to manifest through them, this light, which is love and wisdom, cannot pass through all the layers of impurities they have accumulated from leading their immoderate lifestyle, by not respecting in their intellect and in their heart, the laws of wisdom and love. They must therefore cleanse and purify themselves until their physical, astral, and mental* bodies become so transparent and pure that this divine light, buried within them and struggling to emerge from the darkness, may finally shine in all its brilliance.

* See note and diagram, p. 400 and 401.

19 May

When the chemist pours a few drops of a reagent called 'litmus' into a clear acid solution, the liquid turns red. Then, drop by drop, they add an alkaline solution. At first there is no change. But they continue slowly, drop by drop, and all of a sudden the liquid turns blue. From this phenomenon, we can draw a lesson about psychic life. Someone who transgresses divine laws does not immediately notice the disintegration that occurs within them. They imagine they can continue with impunity... But one day, with just one more transgression, they collapse inwardly.

This law obviously holds true for good as well. Someone comes and complains to me that for years they have worked on themself, without obtaining any result, and they are discouraged. I have to tell them that their reasoning is faulty, because the effects of this work are not immediately visible and tangible. They must continue, and one day, inevitably, the transformation will occur. With good as for evil, you must not imagine that nothing is happening just because, for a long period of time, you do not notice anything.

20 May

*E*ach of you is inhabited by a flame, a divine aspiration, and, although it may be weak, you have the power to feed it so that it becomes an enormous blaze. When you begin to feel this flame burning within you, take care not to expose it to every passing breeze that could extinguish it. In other words, choose carefully the people you associate with, the literature you read, and the entertainment you watch. Choose the best influences for your heart, your mind, your soul and your spirit, influences that strengthen you inwardly.

When you feel you are truly strong and unwavering, you will be able to confront anything, and the same experiences that would have destroyed you before will now strengthen you. When a flame has been given sufficient fuel to become a blaze, no storm can extinguish it. On the contrary, it fans it.

21 May

*O*n departing this earth, it is not only their material possessions that human beings must leave behind. Everything that has come to them in the realms of intelligence and feeling from other people, books, works of art and so on also disappears, unless they have profoundly lived it, experimented with it and verified it. And if they have not done so, when they return in the next incarnation, they will have to learn everything again, and with a great deal of difficulty. Just because someone can speak or write on a variety of subjects is no proof that they truly understand them, and they may have to start all over again from the beginning.

And here is one of the most striking examples. Men and women get married and have children, and many of them feel as helpless and lost in this situation as if they were experiencing it for the first time. Yet how many times have they experienced it in previous incarnations. But since they have never truly sought to deepen their role and their responsibilities as husband, wife, or parent, it is something completely new for them and they make mistakes and suffer. Therefore you must take each role, each activity, seriously so as not to be so helpless in a future incarnation.

22 May

We see roses everywhere, and we give them as gifts, but what is their true significance? Once they have been placed in a vase, we barely notice them or their fragrance when we pass them. However a rose becomes more alive if we look at it with an enlightened consciousness; a contact is established, and you sense that a splendid being lives in this flower and that it speaks to you.

Some will say that it is not possible, that we only read this kind of thing in fairy tales. They will never hear the voice of flowers. In fact there are different ways of hearing the voice of a flower! And if what I am telling you seems to have come from a fairy tale, know that these tales are not merely beautiful stories invented for children by people of great imagination. What is said in fairy tales has a profound reality which you will finally grasp when you open yourself to exchanges with all of nature.

23 May

*M*aster Peter Deunov gave the following rule: 'Use kindness as the basis of your life, justice as balance, wisdom as limit, love as delight, and truth as light.' If we think deeply about this rule, we will find it extremely instructive.

Kindness is the only solid basis on which to build a structure; even if this edifice is beautiful and intelligent, it will collapse if kindness, this benevolence we are capable of showing to all beings, does not support it.

Justice is a quality of balance; to be fair, as illustrated by scales, is knowing how to keep things in balance at all times: don't weigh only on one tray, but make sure a little is added on one side, while a little is subtracted from the other.

Wisdom is a limit, a barrier; that can protect us from external and internal enemies which threaten us.

Love gives us a taste for things; even if we have riches, knowledge and fame, how insipid life would seem without love!

Truth is the light that illuminates our path; thanks to which we move ahead without the risk of losing our way or falling.

24 May

*I*t is natural that everyone is attached to their family, their region, their country and that they work to support them. But that does not prevent them expanding their field of consciousness and thinking much further, much higher. In their heart, in their soul, they must not accept limits. In the same way that you participate in the life of your family, your city, your country, you can learn to participate in cosmic life.

Why do you think you have to be an astronaut in a rocket in order to travel and work in space? The earth travels through the universe, propelled by the sun, and for human beings on earth it is as if they are on a spaceship making its way among the stars. This makes them cosmic citizens capable of participating consciously, luminously, in universal life. This is their true affinity, their true dimension.

25 May

*T*he more sensitive you become, the more likely you are to suffer over all that you see and hear around you. But should we become insensitive in order to avoid suffering? No, with such reasoning, we would quickly become as hard as rock. You must not be afraid to suffer, and particularly in this regard, suffering should not be given much consideration. It is preferable to enhance one's sensitivity, even if we have to suffer, because it is the degree of sensitivity which determines the grandeur and nobility of a human being. You must not, however, confuse sensitivity with sentimentality.

According to initiatic science, to be sensitive is to be able to open oneself more and more to the splendour and wealth of heaven, to capture the marvels of the divine world to the point of barely sensing the stupidity, the vulgarity, and the meanness of human beings. The great masters, and above them the angels and archangels, do not suffer over ugliness; they no longer notice it. They see only beauty, and they live in unceasing joy.

26 May

Jesus said, *'My Father is still working, and I also am working.'* But who, even among the initiates, can pronounce such words? Who even knows what this work is? Most human beings can only say, 'I do odd jobs…I struggle…I rack my brains…I make some feeble attempts.' That is all most humans can say. But real work is something completely different. And this is why, after two thousand years, we have not yet fathomed the deep meaning of the phrase *'My Father is still working, and I also am working.'* It has remained unused and meaningless. Have we ever wondered what this work of God is, how he works, and in what way Jesus was involved in this work?

The work of Christ is to purify, to harmonize and illuminate, and to direct everything toward the divine Source, which in turn pours forth the currents of life over the entire earth. Only someone who has managed to rise as far as the divine Spirit in order to imbue themself with its quintessence and then to distribute its benefits to all creatures, has earned the right to say *'I am working.'*

27 May

A scientist will tell you that only those things which can be observed, calculated, measured, weighed, compared, and classified are real and credible. All the rest is of dubious interest and should be ignored, they say. Very well, but this severely limits the scope of their consciousness, since two-thirds (for the sake of argument, let us say two-thirds) of the life of a human being is taken up by activities which cannot be weighed or measured. Yes, two-thirds of our time is spent living: nothing more.

And if such a life merits no attention and is of no interest, one wonders why a scientist goes on living. Just like other people, they breathe, eat, drink, sleep, and walk; they have thoughts, feelings, sensations, and desires; they meet other people who they like or dislike – they sometimes even hug them – and they do all of this without wondering whether they are doing it scientifically. How can they bear to live a life which is unscientific? They should refuse! Of course it's much better to continue living. But they should take all these manifestations of life seriously, even though, for the time-being, they escape their scientific investigations.

28 May

When you look at the sun, the center of our solar system, try to find the center in you: your spirit – almighty, wise, omniscient, universal love – and draw nearer to it every day! While you remain disconnected from the center, you will be tossed around, at the mercy of the winds and storms that blow throughout the world.

Of course, you will tell me that your daily tasks force you to leave the center to go to your activities at the periphery. Yes, but moving away from the center, when necessary, does not mean cutting the connection with the center. On the contrary, the more activities we have in the world – the periphery – the stronger should be the link with the center, with the spirit. It is from this center that you receive the energy, light and peace you need to carry out these activities. And the sun helps you to maintain the link with the center within you.

29 May

*H*ow many people who lack wisdom and experience imagine they can assume great responsibilities and qualify as authorities! And when they fail, they think they are victims, that others failed to appreciate them, understand them, or support them in their undertaking. Well, this is the worst kind of attitude.

When facing their failures, people must understand that they are not yet ready to realize their ambitions. Even if they are knowledgeable or have a strong will, this is not enough. When they ought to have acted with understanding and attention, they were perhaps closed, hard, and stubborn. When they ought to have been diplomatic and self-controlled, they were perhaps awkward and impatient. Therefore, instead of making the whole world responsible for their failures, they should develop some humility and accept the fact that they have much to learn. It is only from this moment on that success and positive results will be possible for them.

30 May

*I*n your day-to-day life, you will have noticed how often you lack patience! And this lack of patience prevents you from expressing all your good qualities. Every day then, try to develop the ability to bear things more patiently. In other words, instead of immediately reacting to words and events, be quiet inside, breathe deeply, and call upon all the powers of peace, harmony and light for they will help you find a better attitude.

It is important to learn to work with breath! That is also why, when you do the breathing exercises in the morning, you can inwardly repeat the word 'patience' and fill yourself with its meaning, vibration and aura. And as you say this word, add an image that increases its power, until this virtue finally permeates your whole consciousness.

31 May

*C*an we, or even should we continue to love a being who, at a given moment, adopts dishonest and unworthy attitudes and behaviour? Many men and women have had to ask themselves this question. Of course, our love for others always produces certain beneficial effects for them on the subtle planes, and ultimately it can influence them. On the other hand, it is not advisable for our mental balance to carry in our head and in our heart someone who, having taken a wrong turn, is becoming a public danger.

Love must be lived with joy and in the light. And if you feel that a certain man or woman no longer deserves your love, do not persist, there are so many beings on the earth who do, whether you know them or not! It is essential that you never stop loving, because it is love that keeps you alive.

1 June

*T*he notion of royalty necessarily goes hand in hand with that of self-mastery. A monarch who only seeks to impose on others but has not learned to control themself is not really a king or queen, but a slave. A true monarch is someone who first and foremost has become master of themself.

Only a person committed to the ideal of overcoming the domination of their selfish tendencies and to control and orientate their thoughts, feelings and desires, is on the royal road. They inspire respect from all those who come near them because they have not only power but also authority. And then, even the spirits of nature bow at their passing, whispering among themselves, 'Look, a king or queen will be passing by, let's go and welcome them,' and they celebrate. The nature spirits crowd around them because their whole being emanates a fluidic substance of great purity, imbued with soothing and curative influences, felt even by animals, plants and stones.

2 June

*D*o not be ambitious and subject yourself to exhausting rivalries. Choose an activity where you have plenty of space, or are perhaps even alone, for no one will be able to prevent you from growing. If you go and plant yourself beside a great tree, it will complain you are encroaching on its territory. And what will happen if you venture into the territory of a wild animal? Be like a bird instead: it has a tiny little body, fragile and light, with a tiny beak, but it also has wings to fly freely in the air. A bird has no ambition to impose itself on a wild animal; the only thing it asks for from the Creator is its song, joy and freedom of movement.

True sons and daughters of God are like birds; they do not want to clear a path through the jungle, but fly every day in the sky to bring back peace, light and joy, which they then share with all their brothers and sisters.

3 June

*B*lack magic exists, I know, but what I know most of all is that by our way of thinking about objects and events, we increase or diminish their power. Since black magic exists – and even supposing that ill-intentioned people want to use it against us – it is by having faith in its power that we reinforce it. Instead, tell yourself that as a son or daughter of God you cannot be attacked so easily by the forces of evil, and it will not affect you.

But you have to be reasonable. If you suffer a failure, an illness, an accident, or a separation, I urge you not to be hasty to attribute it to black magic. First of all, ask yourself sincerely if the cause is not to be found in yourself instead, and find out what you must do to improve the situation. Do not waste precious time in wild imaginings that will do nothing but aggravate your difficulties and your suffering.

4 June

Someone who strives to act with their soul and spirit, inwardly transforms their difficulties, their suffering. Even if they can do nothing about external events, where others get discouraged and collapse, they find strength, nourishment and the energy to move forward.

Never submit, we must never capitulate, but try to remedy. And to remedy, there is prayer. It is for us to act first. Do not wait for the Lord, in his clemency and mercy, to come and visit us. The Lord will not come down. You might say, 'But we read in the scriptures that on the day of Pentecost, the Holy Spirit descended upon the Apostles in the form of tongues of fire!' In reality, in order to receive the Holy Spirit, a person must first inwardly elevate themselves to the celestial regions, where they merge with the Divinity. And even if we say that the Holy Spirit 'has descended' upon them, on the contrary it is they who have risen up to to it and it has filled them with its presence. The Holy Spirit descends upon us to the extent that we are capable of elevating ourselves.

5 June

What is this 'most powerful force of all forces' about which Hermes Trismegistus speaks in the Emerald Tablet? It is sexual force, since no other force in the universe can compare to it; no other force has the power to create life.

Hermes Trismegistus also says of this force that, 'the sun is its father', which means that sexual energy is of the same nature as solar energy, that it is impregnated with the life, the light and the holiness of the sun. Its use is not therefore limited to procreation; it can also be consecrated to creations of a spiritual order. But how many human beings are ready to admit that this act by which man fertilises woman can become a solar activity?

6 June

A thought has no physical substance, and yet it is not abstract but a real and living being. This is why you must be aware and observe your thoughts.

Thoughts are like children you have to feed, wash and teach. Sometimes, without your realizing, they cling to you, drain your strength and exhaust you. And sometimes these children also escape and roam the world, looting and pillaging as they go. But in the invisible world, as on earth, there is also a police force, and it comes looking for you to make you understand that you are responsible for the damage your children have caused. Then you are taken to court, where you are ordered to pay damages with interest; these payments are your sorrows, your sadness, discouragement and bitterness. So pay attention to your thoughts – do not neglect them. Work to form angelic and heavenly children, who will always accompany you and bring you blessings.

7 June

Much has been said and written about initiations, because at different times and in different places on earth they have taken very different forms. The fact is that all initiations, past as well as present, wherever they take place, have only one goal: to unite spirit and matter. Yes, one goal only: the fusion of spirit and matter, one could also say, of human beings and their Creator.

You will ask, 'But then, if it is only to achieve this single goal, why are the explanations and methods for reaching it so varied and numerous?' It is because the knowledge necessary to realize this fusion is infinite. Human beings must place all their means and all the knowledge they ceaselessly work to acquire, in the service of this one goal: to unite with the Divinity, to become one with the first Cause. For as long as they seek something other than that, they will simply wander along paths that lead them nowhere.

8 June

What is harmful for some can be harmless or even beneficial for others. Some creatures are so familiar with fire that they are not burned. Snake venom is deadly for human beings, while on certain animals it has no effect. Put still more simply, some people cannot tolerate the air (they catch cold) or the light (it irritates their eyes), and yet there is nothing better than air and light.

It can be said, then, that anything human beings consider to be evil is not necessarily so. It may be disturbing and threatening to them for the time being, because they are still weak or ill. What they express about it thus reflects only their personal views and their resilience; it is a very relative judgement. But ask the initiates and their response will surprise you: because they have learned to make use of evil, it has become an asset for them. And how? They transform it.

9 June

*I*n the book of Genesis it is written that on the sixth day God created humankind and that he created them in his image. But there are very few people, even among Jews and Christians who have heard this passage so often, that take seriously the idea of the sublime future that awaits humankind. So what do they make of this basic truth revealed in their Holy Scriptures?

If humankind was created in the image of God, we must be logical and accept the consequences. And indeed, one of the consequences is that despite all their imperfections and weaknesses, they are promised a heavenly and sublime future. We have no right to limit the extent of this truth, because otherwise, what future do we envisage for the image of God?

10 June

You can have plans, you can make wishes, but life is such that you can never be sure of anything, not of events and even less of human beings. And it is pointless to bemoan the fact: it is so. You may say that you need to count on the love you receive from your parents, from your friends and those around you. That is true, but you must know that while they will sometimes think of you, quite often they will also forget you, because they have their own worries and their own preoccupations. So, do not count so much on them, and understand that it is within yourself that you must establish something stable.

Yes, we must learn to know the nature of things and to understand what we should do to avoid one disappointment after another. Since you need love in order to be happy, since you feel it is love that makes you flourish, that provides revelations, and since you want your love to last forever, well then, love, but do not wait to be loved. If those who are dear to you respond to your love and your trust, well and good, give thanks to heaven, but do not count on it. It is only in this way that you will always feel free.

11 June

*H*eaven does not require that people be perfect, only that they work to perfect themselves. One day everyone should be able to say, 'Now I must sow seeds in my soul – luminous thoughts, the love of a high ideal – and I shall continue to watch over them, to warm them, water them, and nourish them with all that is best in me. I know that the universe is governed by laws, and that according to one of these laws, every seed eventually produces fruit, so I try to sow only the best seeds.' And this is truly to have faith: to be convinced that every seed sown in the soil of your soul will bear fruit.

So, whatever religion you may belong to – Christianity, Islam, Judaism, Hinduism, Buddhism, or any other – until you understand this universal law and apply it in your life, you do not possess faith but only beliefs, which cannot get you very far. Rather, they can take you a long way, but it is down the road of laziness, failure, discouragement, rebellion, and so on.

12 June

So many tragedies are caused by people who claim to work for good, and yet cannot respond reasonably when faced with a minor offence or injustice! They mean well, but at the slightest provocation they create interminable conflict.

Most conflicts originate as miniscule incidents which, instead of being dealt with as they could have been, because they were not dealt with right away, assumed undue importance and eventually escalated. We know this, but do we draw lessons for the future? Do we ask ourselves, 'If I adopt a certain attitude, if I make a certain decision, will my contribution improve matters or complicate them further?' We have to wonder whether human beings truly desire good. If they did, they would succeed in achieving it. And in any case, it would be easier for them to put out a small fire at the beginning, instead of having to control a big fire which their intransigence and unwillingness had allowed to spread.

13 June

We listen in wonder when some people speak: they express themselves with such intelligence, such clarity, such eloquence! But, in fact, it is not enough to understand things intellectually and to explain brilliantly what you have understood; your understanding must manifest in every realm of your existence.

Someone says, 'I understand, I understand...' All right, but if they really understood, they should act according to what they understood. But for most people, there is a world between understanding and achievement. They understand that we must be honest, sincere, forgiving, altruistic ... and that is enough for them; how they then behave, that's another question! Well, they still have to learn that true understanding is never separated from achievement. Someone who does not express by their actions what they claim to have understood, has not really understood. If they had understood, they would have achieved. Because knowledge is power. If you cannot achieve, you do not yet understand: so strive to acquire the missing elements of your knowledge that you need in order to achieve.

14 June

When you are faced with a problem or receive unpleasant news, observe your reactions. Right away, an entire internal mechanism is set in motion: you become anxious, you imagine the worst and, as a result, through no-one's fault but your own, what began as a small pebble becomes an enormous rock that obstructs your path. It is senseless.

In future, be careful: the moment you receive unpleasant news, and are faced with a bad surprise, instead of giving way immediately to anger, despondency or grief, stop and say, 'I'll wait, it may not be so serious, things will work out…'. In doing so, instead of blowing this event out of all proportion and being crushed even before things happen, you reinforce yourself. Why do you always expect things to turn out badly, and for the worst?

15 June

The syllable Om corresponds to what – in the Western tradition – we call the Logos, the Word of creation. In the Hindu tradition, it represents the original sound and is associated with Kalahamsa, this cosmic bird that laid the primordial egg from which the universe was born.

Om is a syllable with very powerful vibrations which Hindus use as a mantra. They repeat it untiringly in their meditations. You too can pronounce this mantra either aloud or mentally. You can concentrate on this word without thinking of anything else and repeat, Om, Om, Om... You can also associate it with a breathing exercise. Inhale through the nose while mentally pronouncing Om four times, then exhale very slowly through the mouth while repeating Om. After a while, you will feel calmer and full of energy.

The syllable Om can also be decomposed as Aum, and it is in this form that we sing it. If we are conscious of the magical power of sounds, we can gradually feel what perfect forms this song produces in our soul.

16 June

On the pretext of protecting their independence and freedom, many people refuse to participate in the collective life. Well, these people do not realize to what extent they are actually limiting themselves. Like children they move within the small circle of their feelings, their desires, and their greed. What poverty, what misery! This limited state is normal for a child, but not for an adult.

Adults must show that they are able to think of others: their family first, of course, but also their neighbours, friends, colleagues, and fellow citizens. And even then, this is limited. The circle must become wider and wider, to include country, race*, the whole of humanity, and still further, to encompass the universe, infinity... Rare are those who have reached beyond all these limitations, whose desires, thoughts, and interests converge on the collective, universal aspect of life. It is in this direction that we must strive.

* For decades, genetic research has shown that the notion of 'race' has no solid base : despite the difference in traits, skin colour and so on, there is only one human species. It is therefore advisable to avoid using this term in speeches and texts. Nevertheless, almost daily, the media echo insults and 'racial' violence, tensions and riots. This is unfortunate, but until individuals cease to believe that they can persecute their fellow humans thanks to their 'racial' group, this is a term that we will have to keep. (Note from the editor).

*D*o not seek clairvoyance through occult methods. True clairvoyance, the true eyes, are in the heart, and it is love which opens these eyes. A woman who loves a man sees things in him that no one else sees. And if she sees him as a divinity, do not tell her she is mistaken! Objectively speaking, yes, she is mistaken; but if she seems to exaggerate the beauty and virtues of her beloved, it is because she sees him as God originally created him, or as he will be when he returns to the womb of the Eternal.

You have not yet understood the power of love to open the eyes of the soul. Those of you who wish to become clairvoyant must learn to love. Your hearts must call out for help, like the blind man in the Gospels: *'Have pity on us, Lord.'* Launch an appeal, and one day the light of the cosmos will come and ask you, 'What can I do for you?' 'That my eyes may be opened!' You will be heard: your eyes will be opened.

18 June

You have a tree in your garden: you can pass it several times a day without paying it any attention, as if it were a piece of stage set made from plaster or cardboard. But you can also be conscious that it is a living being, and you can even approach it, greet it, talk to it, and absorb what it represents.

You may say, 'Greet a tree, talk to it, what good can that do?' Of course, physically and materially, this changes nothing. But, on the subtle planes, the tree is enriched by your presence and, at the same time, you are enriched by it. It is you, in fact, who gains the most: you enter into communication with the life that circulates from the roots all the way to the tips of its branches, and you also become acquainted with the invisible creatures who live in it and look after it. Yes, for there are beings who work to maintain life everywhere in nature.

A person who falls in love has no doubts about what they feel, even though they cannot see or touch their love, for feelings are impalpable. And someone who holds an opinion and has convictions, can they see them or touch them? No, and yet sometimes they are willing to fight and die for them. And someone who says, 'Upon my soul and conscience, I condemn this man', passes a sentence heavy with consequences, in the name of something they too have never seen. Why do they suddenly attach such importance to this invisible soul and conscience?

Without realising it, humans believe only in what is invisible and impalpable: everyone feels, loves, suffers, cries and celebrates for reasons that are invisible. And yet certain claim to believe only in what they can see and touch! What a contradiction!

20 June

When we read the lives of the saints, the prophets and the initiates, we find that all of them have undergone terrible ordeals. Those who understood their meaning were not discouraged and did not rebel; they knew that it was thanks to this hardship that they would become divinities. But others who had not yet gained sufficient light were overwhelmed and sometimes even rebelled: why did heaven not come to their aid? They had sacrificed everything for it, and now they were being abandoned!

What spiritualists often lack is true knowledge. Because they have consecrated their life to God, they imagine they will see streams flowing with milk and honey, that they will receive white robes and crowns etc. It is true that such promises are found in the Bible, and it is also true that this will come to be, but only when they have passed every test! In the meantime, whatever their difficulties may be, those who possess true light must learn to use it for their evolution.

21 June

Why do we watch the sunrise? Why do we concentrate on it? In order to learn to mobilize all our thoughts, all our desires, and all our energies, and to direct them toward the realization of the highest ideal.

A person who works to unify the many chaotic forces that pull them in every direction and to project them in a single, luminous and life-giving direction becomes such a powerful centre that their presence, like the sun, is able to radiate through space. Yes, those who manage to control the tendencies of their lower nature can spread these blessings over the whole of humanity, and become a sun. They live in such freedom that they expand the field of their consciousness so that all may benefit from the abundance of light and love that pour forth from them.

22 *June*

*B*y means of gestures, words, facial expressions, and clothes, a person makes an effort to be presentable when they go out to meet others. But when they are alone at home, they let themself go, because no one can see them. But are they really alone? No, they are inhabited by an entire population, by their cells which are living and intelligent entities. This populace observes them, and its scrutiny is much more severe than that of society, because it is not impressed with their carefully studied clothes or gestures, but with who they are, deep down.

So think more often about these citizens within you because if they feel you are allowing yourself to become inwardly lazy, sensual, unstable or violent, they say, 'Since our master is setting us this example, we are going to imitate him, and he shall see what he shall see!' And they rebel, not only in your psychic body but also in your physical body. On the contrary, however, if you know how to set a good example for them, this community is capable of working wonders.

23 *June*

*F*or most human beings, everyday life is made up of turmoil, complaints, struggles and bitterness. Why? Because their field of consciousness is so narrow and limited that nothing seems more important to them than their worries, their ambitions, their desires and their quarrels. They do not see the immensity of the sky above them, all this infinite space. If they decided to look up, they would tear themselves free of these limitations, and they would begin to breathe freely again. Yes, it is only a question of the direction in which you are looking: not so much downward, but more upwared.

Those who think of infinity and eternity begin to feel that they soar above everything, that nothing can touch them anymore – no misfortune, no insult, no loss – because a new consciousness is beginning to awaken within them.

24 June

When faced with the truths of spiritual science, some people simply take on an air of suspicion and insinuation. They say, 'Personally, I doubt that… I am a sceptic', as if this scepticism were the fruit of many years of deep reflection. In fact, the opposite is true. They show how limited they are intellectually: they have not studied, nor do they wish to make the effort, so they find it convenient to remain in doubt. This spares them the trouble of true reflection and creates the illusion that they are great thinkers.

Someone who describes themself as a sceptic only reveals that they have never studied anything in depth. Yes, if they have failed to acquire certitude, it is because they have not gone far enough in their research. It also shows that they are arrogant and pretentious, since they attribute no value to all the knowledge that others, who came before them, had worked so hard to acquire and make available to us.

25 June

*H*uman intelligence is a manifestation of Cosmic Intelligence, but a very imperfect one; for in passing through minds and hearts which are continually prey to disordered passions, it is limited and obscured. Cosmic Intelligence cannot manifest perfectly through a being who does not know how to control their instinctual movements. The more they learn to control and purify themself, the better channel they are for this Intelligence.

The intelligence of a human being is not only the product of their studies and reflections; it depends on the good or bad state of all the cells in their body. They must pay careful attention to the quality of their physical food, but more importantly to the quality of their psychic food – their sensations, feelings, desires and thoughts, or they will remain closed to the greatest revelations. The only way to improve one's intelligence is to improve one's way of life. The initiates have always believed this; they have always known it and worked accordingly.

26 June

In whatever state you find yourself, even the most dire, be courageous, because a great inheritance, a divine legacy awaits you. If until now you have not yet taken possession of it, it is because you are still a minor. It is not possible to know exactly when, but it is certain that you will receive your inheritance when you reach adulthood. It may be in twenty or thirty year's time, or perhaps in another incarnation. You might say, 'But how will they find me? I will be living in a different country, and will have a different nationality.' You can change anything you want: the celestial entities will always find you.

Therefore, every day, think about this divine heritage, and this thought alone will act most favourably on you.

Nothing promised to human beings will ever satisfy the immensity of their desires. A wife or a husband, a house, a little garden, a car... what are they? Even when people have acquired them all, they are still dissatisfied. Immensity, infinity, and eternity, this is our true heritage, the only one capable of fulfilling our heart's desire.

27 June

*I*n order to know love, to feel love, to live love and to give love, we must work toward the harmonious development of our intellect, our heart and our will.

True love is not just a state of feeling, true love is a state of consciousness, the highest that a human being can attain. It is divine consciousness in all its fullness, and it is not given to everyone to experience it, in fact it is quite rare. Those who are touched by this love, even for an instant, feel as if they have been struck by lightning. Suddenly they receive something so sublime that they almost cannot bear it, but it is this love which enlightens them – which vivifies and reawakens them. Even if we liken it again to a flash of lightning, this consciousness bears no relation to what we generally call love, which is most often just a jumble of confused emotions. True love involves our entire being.

28 June

It is not enough to know the methods that enable you to become a clairvoyant, a magus, an alchemist and so on. You must first of all ask yourself what goal you are working towards and understand that there are laws to be respected. Those who practise occult methods for their personal benefit violate the laws of cosmic harmony, and in the end the cosmos itself vetoes their plans, and they fail miserably.

Many occultists or so-called spiritualists have ended in disaster, because they worked to accomplish certain things without first finding out whether they were acting in harmony with the plans of Cosmic Intelligence. Books on occult sciences suggest a great many techniques and rituals, but apart from the fact that many of these practices are risky, not one of them is as valuable as harmonising ourselves with the cosmic order. And this is not all: even the most inoffensive practices become dangerous and backfire in the hands of those who do not work to preserve this harmony, and who allow their anarchic tendencies to get the upper hand.

29 June

*S*uffering gives human beings an opportunity to enter into themselves to think, meditate and attract superior beings who will guide and help them. There is no greater science than to know how to suffer. Someone who knows how to suffer gives off the perfume of flowers. Distilling and exhaling perfume is the science of flowers. Because they have learned to withstand bad weather and survive in spite of all the dangers that threaten them, flowers give off an exquisite scent, and we love them for it.

But what fragrance is given off by those who scream and protest at the slightest pain or annoyance? Only one who has learned to accept their suffering distils this perfume. An initiate suffers when they have taken the burdens and sins of human beings upon themself, as Jesus did. This suffering that has been consented to with love, produces the most exquisite scent; and angels come to delight in its presence, just as we too rejoice over a blossoming tree in a garden.

Just as animals have to eat to survive, human beings must eat too, but they should not content themselves with eating like an animal, in other words without consciousness. Why? Because food is not a dead substance, it has a voice, it speaks to us, it passes on its secrets to us. To receive these secrets we must learn to eat in silence and to concentrate on each mouthful of food we are eating.

Food is condensed sunlight and also condensed sounds because light is not separate from sound. To people who are attentive, who have practised hearing it, light speaks, it sings, it is music, it is the divine Word. In today's noisy world we cannot hear anything, and that is a great shame. To understand the language of food, we must begin by restoring silence, not only around us, but also within us.

1 July

*T*he circle with the point in the centre is a structure which is found everywhere in the universe. It is that of the solar system, with the sun in its centre. And, at the other end of the scale, it is also that of the cell, which is composed of a nucleus, a substance called cytoplasm, and surrounding it, a skin or membrane. An analogous structure is also found in the egg (made up of the yolk, the white, and the shell) and also in most fruits (with the stone or the seeds, the flesh and the skin). All living organisms are made up of a centre, then a space in which life circulates, and finally a 'skin' which serves as a barrier, a boundary. The space surrounding the point represents matter. Matter is indisscociable from the notion of space, whereas spirit is like a single point. And spirit's power lies in the fact that, although it is an imperceptible entity, it is active everywhere at the same time.

2 July

We are at times struck by the faces of those who have had to confront the intrigues, attacks and betrayals of those around them and have successfully overcome their hardships: their eyes and their expressions manifest the wealth of their inner life. They have lost almost nothing; or, to use an image from the world of banking, they have lost only the interest for now, but their capital remains intact.

Observe and compare those who give in completely to their disappointments and discouragement with those who succeed in overcoming them. What a difference! Those who surrender to discouragement and bitterness have lost their true wealth, whereas the others win it back a hundredfold, a thousandfold: they are vivacious and enthusiastic, and they are always ready to get back to work.

3 July

*I*t is necessary to treat physical illnesses with physical remedies, but that is not sufficient. Illness is often caused indirectly by some mistakes we have made in not knowing how to control thoughts, feelings or desires. As a result, if we do not seek to remedy these aspects, we cannot be healed permanently. The solution is to use all the resources medicine has to offer and at the same time address the emotional and mental aspects of the problem in order to eliminate the causes.

Therefore, take the medicine and undergo the treatment if necessary. But you must also accompany the treatment with work on the psyche, because with time thoughts and feelings eventually affect matter and take part in its transformation. This is true medicine. Taking medicines will always be more effective if supported by the power of your thought and the strength of your love.

4 July

*H*uman beings are capable of great things, but only if they begin with the small things; and the greater their ambition, the more modestly they must begin. Those who are successful sense their consciousness expanding, and it is this expansion of consciousness that matters as it provides a foundation and support for the future. On the other hand, setting one's sights too high can only lead to failure, and this failure diminishes something within and undermines confidence.

When you engage in the spiritual life, do not begin by saying, 'In some months, or a few years, I will have overcome all my bad tendencies and live in divine light'. This is not possible. Why? Because these are tendencies which you have nurtured over many incarnations and, if you think you will be able to overcome them in a short period of time, you will be faced with failure and will soon become discouraged.

5 July

*E*very day, we hear human beings repeating, 'Oh! What a world we live in! There is so much selfishness and dishonesty. Injustice always wins out. Whatever we do to improve the situation, we'll never succeed.' By their attachment to such negative thoughts they are constantly inviting them to their table, 'Come, come, there is plenty of food here for you.' Well, this is a very dangerous attitude. By endlessly emphasising evil and continually focusing on it, they do nothing to diminish it; on the contrary, they encourage and reinforce it.

From now on, therefore, you must encourage the good by saying, 'Come, angels, come; heavenly entities, give us your wisdom, your love, and your strength, so that every day we may do something good here on earth.'

6 July

When you listen to music, think of using it in your spiritual work. Music creates an atmosphere. It can also be compared to the wind filling the sails of a ship and pushing it towards new horizons: to the realization of your ideal and your highest aspirations.

Observe yourself when you listen to music: you feel uplifted and inclined to let your mind drift. Instead, try to focus your thoughts, on what you most ardently want to achieve. If you have a meeting with someone or have some work to complete, well, you can consciously prepare yourself for this meeting or this work by listening to music. If you seek wisdom, love and beauty, imagine that music lifts you up to the spiritual regions where you will find these qualities in abundance. Sound is a force that propels you, but it's up to you to choose the direction in which you wish to be taken.

7 July

*I*t is often said that hope keeps us alive. When human beings are dissatisfied with their lot or disappointed by events, they tend to project their hopes into the future, 'Soon... in a few days... in a few months... things will get better.' There is no doubt that hope is the very last thing to be abandoned, but while we hang on, waiting for things to get better, we need to count on something reliable. In order to hang on, we need to have faith. And faith relies on the conviction that the universe is governed by laws, and in particular the law according to which all seeds eventually bear fruit: if we have sown good seeds, we will one day harvest magnificent fruit. But we must also cultivate life within us and be energized by our love. For otherwise, hope will simply be a means to escape when faced with reality, and will also, one day, abandon us.

If we do not want to lose hope, we must keep faith and love forever alive within us and call on them for help whenever difficulties arise. This will enable us to keep hope to the very end.

8 July

What is more visible and more radiant than the sun? But if you remain barricaded behind closed shutters, you will not even know that it exists. If you want to see it, you must at least open a window. The sun is not going to impose itself on you by penetrating your walls and shutters. In the same way, you must at least open a small skylight within you in order to discover the presence of God. Yes, it is you who must do something, not God.

God is there in his radiance, and this should be enough for you. It is up to you to do what is necessary to feel his presence. Those who have evolved to a higher degree of consciousness never cease to have revelations on the meaning and beauty of the world, so how could they help but feel this divine presence? This is what God is, and we gradually discover him as we come to know the richness and meaning of life.

9 July

Truth will never present itself as something so obvious that it imposes itself on us; neither is it something we can impose on others. It is we who, through an ordered and sensible psychic life, are capable of coming closer to the truth. Perhaps we will never attain it, but in seeking to perfect ourselves each day, we come closer to it.

So when certain believers glory in belonging to the one true religion, this does not mean that they themselves live the truth. A certificate of baptism does not guarantee possession of the truth. It is the efforts they make every day to wrest themselves from their weaknesses that is most important: this is the only sign that they belong to the true religion.

10 July

Why is it so important to live in harmony? Because it is a state which activates a series of physical and chemical reactions in the body, as a result of which all our physiological processes function more effectively. To live in harmony means that one has decided to experiment with the power of the spirit, of the soul, of thought, and of feeling, on the physical body.

How many people ruin their health because they endlessly nourish chaotic thoughts and emotions! They have not understood that these are malevolent forces which are destroying them, and they continue to seek the cause of their sickness elsewhere. When will they understand that it is often their thoughts and feelings that are making them ill? When they stop feeding them and try to introduce harmony within, by breathing it in and immersing themselves in it, they will immediately feel better.

11 July

*I*n whatever domain it may be, all scientific progress has taken place only because human beings have discovered that the physical world obeys certain laws. But people want to think of the psychic or moral world as a realm of the greatest chaos and anarchy where there are no laws to be understood or rules to be respected! Well, this is not possible. And if by their rash or unconscious behaviour human beings upset the extraordinary mechanism of their psychic organism, they do irreparable damage.

Nothing is stable or reliable when we fail to respect these laws, because they constitute the framework of the universe – the psychic as well as the physical universe. Failure to recognise these laws is the greatest mistake. We behave as if they were a human invention, as if they rested on arbitrary and questionable foundations and can be transgressed without serious consequence. Not at all! Nothing and no one will be able to help those who transgress the laws of the psychic and spiritual worlds.

12 July

We should ideally do our morning gymnastic and breathing exercises every day in nature so as to benefit from the purest air possible, since it's from the air that we can harness this precious quintessence the Indian yogis called prana. Prana is life energy that exists everywhere, in the earth, in water, air and fire, but it is mainly carried by the sun's rays, and is most abundant in the early morning. Each particle of this prana is like a drop of crystalline water, a tiny, suspended sphere of light filled with a spiritual essence. And we can capture some of these drops of light through our breathing.

By consciously passing the air through our nostrils, we set our subtle centres in motion and they work to extract the quintessence from the air. Once it has been captured, this quintessence circulates; it is like fire running through the network of nerves on either side of our spine. Just as blood circulates though veins, arteries and capillaries, prana circulates throughout our nervous system. Not only does our physical health depend on our nervous system, but so do the development of our spiritual faculties and the awakening of our chakras.

13 July

*J*ust because you eventually admit that hardships are useful does not mean you must go looking for them. In any case, you can be sure that they will come looking for you, because no-one on earth is sheltered from hardships. Above all, do not try to imitate those who are prepared to accomplish heroic acts despite the dangers, but who cannot tolerate the slightest inconveniencies in their daily life that they consider to be beneath them: they only make life unbearable for those around them.

Not everyone is destined to be a hero. On the other hand, everyone must strive humbly to accept and surmount the difficulties which face them every day. This is the only way to avoid even greater suffering. When we fail to make these efforts, the slightest hardships become truly insurmountable.

14 July

You have all heard of 'double agents', men and women who serve their own country and the enemies of their country at the same time. They think they will always have a safe haven, whatever happens. And in so many businesses as well, we see people serving both the interests of their employer and those of their competitors! Such double-dealing is very detrimental both for the countries and the companies, but also for the individuals themselves who, in the end, risk rejection by both sides.

This attitude is also widespread in the spiritual life. How many people unconsciously serve both God, and what in the Gospel Jesus calls Mammon (wealth) at the same time; that is to say, both the powers of heaven, the spirit, and those of the earth and physical matter? Each one of us must become conscious of this, because such duplicity is very dangerous and is a threat of spiritual death. That is why Jesus said, *'You cannot serve God and wealth'*.

15 July

*M*arriage is not a human institution, or more precisely, it is human institution that reproduces a cosmic phenomenon: that of a marriage first celebrated on high between the heavenly Father and his wife, the divine Mother. And because human beings have been created in the image of God, they repeat this cosmic event in an instinctive but also unfortunately in an unconscious manner.

Christianity is still a long way from understanding this truth. For Christians, God is uniquely a masculine principle. Well, no, they are mistaken. If man seeks woman to unite with her and create, it is because they reproduce a model: God also has a wife with whom he unites in order to create. His wife is the divine Mother, Nature, Cosmic Matter. The law is absolute: everything which is below is like that which is above. Therefore, everything which takes place below is in the image of that which takes place on high. And God's wife is a magnificent reality that exists as a principle.

16 July

It is possible to escape human justice, but it is impossible to escape divine justice. Why? Because these two forms of justice are not of the same nature. Divine justice cannot touch human beings externally, but it touches them inwardly. There are criminals who have always managed to escape human justice, but inwardly they are being destroyed: their health, their psychic state, everything is falling apart. On the face of things certain elements are still holding up, but gradually they will disintegrate, because it is the inner realm that nourishes them and that sustains the edifice; and if the inner realm collapses, then the outer realms will also soon fall. This is how divine justice makes itself known. And even if its sanctions are not immediately visible, they are instantaneous: the moment a human being makes a transgression, something in them darkens, something starts to disintegrate. Even if it takes years for this disintegration to appear externally, it has already started inwardly.

17 July

*A*ll those who have understood what spiritual life truly is become like gardens and orchards where all sorts of fruit ripen. The divine gardeners, the celestial entities come to visit and exclaim, 'Oh! This cantaloupe, this watermelon, this peach... what magnificent fruits! Quick, let's taste them!' Yes, when they see a being that has finally awakened to the spiritual life, they care for them and delight in everything that emanates from their heart and soul. Every woman, every man can be visited by these heavenly gardeners.

Someone might say, 'But I have nothing to give, I am not an orchard, so why would they come and seek something from me?' In reality, there is always some useful element to be extracted... even from poisonous plants, if only to make medicines. This is why, even if they do not suspect it, human beings are always visited by creatures from other worlds. And if they persist in producing poison, certain entities will approach to gather substances which they will perhaps turn into vaccines!

18 July

True silence can be defined as the highest region of our soul. The moment we reach this region, we enter into cosmic light.

Light is the quintessence of the universe. It passes through and permeates everything we see around us – people, nature, objects and even what we cannot see. The silence we strive to create within us during concentration, meditation and prayer has only one goal: fusion with this primal light which is vibrant and powerful, and which penetrates all of creation.

19 July

*U*ntil men and women rediscover the meaning of the sublimation of sexual energy, they will be disappointed with their love experiences. When they feel desire, a mutual attraction, why do they immediately want to satisfy it? Why do they not try to acquire the control that could make them beings that are luminous and powerful? Of course it is difficult, but if they start to get into the habit of mastering themselves, they will gradually be able to use this urge to release within themselves forces of a subtler nature that will open their heart and make their thoughts more penetrating; they will discover such wealth in themselves and in all other beings that they could never have imagined until then.

For a certain time at least, when men and women meet, they should be content to marvel at each other while giving thanks to the divine Mother and heavenly Father for the energy given to them. They will thus experience states of consciousness of great poetry and elevation, and life will seem much more beautiful.

Why continue to uphold the belief that God punishes humans for their errors? Whatever their mistakes may be, human beings are neither forsaken nor punished by God. It is they who, through their errors, turn away from him, and in doing so they encounter nothing but cold, darkness and limitations of every kind; it is they themselves who have put themselves into this sad predicament.

People reason as if their actions were exterior to themselves and could be detached from them. No, these actions, whether good or evil, and even if the effects are felt externally to them, leave traces mainly within them, and these traces are indelible. So, if they wish to feel divine benevolence and love once more, there is only one solution: they must become conscious of their mistakes and strive to correct them.

21 July

The sun's rays are forces which influence everything they penetrate, because they are inhabited by living entities. Their different manifestations correspond to different colours: red, orange, yellow, green, blue, indigo and violet, of which white light is the synthesis. When these rays are projected onto living beings, they work on them.

Initiates use light and colours to help human beings and they teach their disciples to work on themselves with light and colour. Each colour corresponds to a virtue, and this explains why each mistake you make reduces the force within you that corresponds to one of these colours. Since time immemorial the initiates have worked with light, for it is light alone that bestows true power and real knowledge. With the laser, official science is gradually discovering the extraordinary power of light, but the powers of spiritual light are far greater still.

22 July

Learn to nourish yourself with the scent of flowers without picking them, for the flower you pick is already dead. God had put this flower in his garden where it was radiant and free. But, you wanted to put it in a vase in your home or in your buttonhole so that everyone could see the flower belonged to you. Why? Are you not content with being able to smell its perfume?

Of course, the flowers I am talking about are purely symbolic. Flowers represent human beings, men and women, and the scent is their emanations, their light, warmth and poetic nature that radiates from them. No-one will criticize you for wanting to enjoy this scent; it is there for everyone to smell and in particular for those who are able to appreciate it. If, however, you picked the flower to take it away with you, you would be responsible for making the flower wilt and dry out. It was planted in God's soil; why should you uproot it?

23 July

*I*n the physical realm, human beings have made gigantic achievements: we cannot help but see how scientific and technical progress has transformed life. But this is not enough, and humanity is now called upon to realize achievements that are still more important, more vital for them, by of the faculties of the spirit. Through meditation and prayer, they must learn to make a relationship with the world of the spirit, so that light, love, and power of the spirit descend upon the earth, within them, and upon those beings around them.

Scientific and technical progress has limits, and even presents dangers. If all these discoveries are not made to serve a higher vision of things, humanity will be overwhelmed, overtaken and crushed by them. Scientific and technical achievements are not sufficient to transform life. It is by means of the spirit that life will be truly transformed, because peace, freedom, and brotherhood are accomplishments of the spirit.

24 July

How do most countries believe they can solve problems with their neighbours and ensure their safety? By perfecting weapons which are more and more deadly... Until one day they will end up destroying the whole earth. Because, with this approach, as time passes, things become more complicated. Until human beings choose to solve their problems with spiritual force, with the power of divine love, nothing will ever be resolved.

Therefore, whatever your situation and station in life may be, from this day forward you at least must try to resolve any problems with your parents, your friends or your enemies by expressing love and kindness. By doing so, you will activate a law which will require them sooner or later to respond in the same way. Yes, this is the power of provocation. Until you understand how to resolve problems, you will provoke the negative side in others, which in turn will wait until you drop your guard and then come back to attack you. Study history and you will see that this has always been the case. From now on, learn to provoke the good in all those you meet.

25 July

*A*n initiate does not speak only with words; his language can be compared to that of nature. What does nature do? It sends us messages all the time. It does not use words, and yet it speaks to us: the sun, stars, forests, lakes, oceans, and mountains speak to us by constantly communicating something of their life and their secrets. These communications are recorded within us, but we are not conscious of them. Yet, it is thanks to them that little by little our sensitivity is enriched and our understanding enhanced. We do not know how this understanding comes about, but it does.

An initiate's language is identical to that of nature. Thanks to the power of his spirit, he emits particles, he projects rays, and, consciously or unconsciously, those who receive them are enlightened and enriched.

26 July

*I*t is essential to have the correct attitude toward all that exists and, above all, toward the First Cause, the Creator. When you have a positive attitude toward the Creator, wherever you go, all of creation, all creatures from the angels to the birds, the trees and the mountains, will look at you and smile. New forces and new joys will come to visit you, and you will go forward with confidence that life is beautiful and has meaning.

Heavenly beings will never bow before your power, your wealth, your knowledge or your prestige; they will only open themselves up to you if they feel you have the right attitude, for only your attitude reveals whether you have understood what is essential. Never forget this truth: everything that happens in your life from then on will provide opportunities for you to verify it.

27 July

When you go walking in nature, whether it is in the countryside, in the forest, in the mountains or at the sea-side, be aware of the space surrounding you and from time to time, stop and breathe in deeply in order to contact the Angel of air.

The Angel of air is a living and intelligent entity, and you can therefore ask, 'O beloved Angel of air, you who are a servant of God who is great and almighty, blow through me and clear out the impurities from my lungs, heart and brain, and bring me harmony so that I can become a servant like you.' And because the Angel of air is present everywhere and directs all the currents circulating throughout the universe and slips into every crack, he hears you. He then gives the spirits accompanying him the order to bring you some breaths of this very subtle fluid we call ether, and you feel as if your entire being is expanding and rising into space.

28 July

Your salvation lies in your ability to recognise your divine lineage, to become conscious that God is within you, that he lives in you and that you can therefore identify with him. But of course this exercise requires that you take certain precautions. First of all, your consciousness that the divinity dwells within you must be accompanied by the same consciousness that the divinity lives in all human beings as well. In this way, you will remain humble, simple, amiable, and open to others.

What is more, in doing this exercise of identification, do not begin to think that you are equal to God, as did Lucifer and the rebel angels, according to the tradition. Instead, make efforts to sense that it is not you who exist, but that God alone exists, and that he exists within you only in so far as your ceaseless efforts enable him to manifest through your thoughts, your feelings, and your acts.

29 July

Why is the brain situated at the top of the body? If you understood the reason, you would not remain down below in your heart and your emotions, suffering in self-pity, when you experience disappointment and unhappiness. You would immediately force yourself to rise higher, to the level of true thought, of reason and intelligence.

When you are suffering and distressed, say to yourself, 'You are right, I understand, and I am going to get the handkerchiefs ready to wipe away your tears. But wait a bit, I need to do a little thinking first.' And in reflecting, you find the solution much more rapidly than if you had continued to stumble around in that part of you that is so sensitive: the astral body. Otherwise, what happens? You complain, you cry for hours, stopping only because you are worn out. And the next day you begin again. But your tears and lamentations solve nothing. So, instead of remaining below in your feelings, why not force yourself to move out right away and take up residence on high, in the spiritual realm which is pure reason and where the spirit reigns?

30 July

Most men and women are so careless when they enter a relationship or marriage! They imagine that everything will be easy, light and pleasant, since their partner is there, of course, merely to satisfy their desires and for them to live happy moments. But gradually they begin to feel that it's not that easy and then come the arguments and confrontations, until they understand that, in order to restore the situation, they must each strive to forget themselves a little and think of the other. What they mistook for a romantic adventure or a fairy tale, is in fact a school where they begin what for every human being is the most important apprenticeship: the expansion of consciousness.

Perhaps you are wondering what this expansion of consciousness entails. It means leaving one's small, egocentric self in order to enter the vast community of humanity; and for many, this apprenticeship inevitably begins with the experience called 'falling in love'.

31 July

The work you do once you are engaged in the spiritual life is very different from everything you are used to. It is not a matter of doing manual work somewhere or being busy in an office, but of developing the divine nature given to us by our heavenly Father and which is stifled and buried in everyday life by all sorts of activities and preoccupations which are not really divine.

It is a waste of time to go to an initiatic school with the idea of carrying out the same activities there as you do in the world: you will feel alone and even rejected, not so much by the people you will meet there, but by the very atmosphere of the school – you will have the feeling you're in a foreign land. But if you wish to find the right conditions to restore order and harmony within yourselves, to allow your divine nature to blossom, and to undertake great work for the good of the whole world, you must turn to an initiatic school where you will always accepted and welcomed!

1 August

*S*piritual life should not be embarked upon rashly, because you can get lost in it just as much as you can get lost at sea without a compass. Although in spiritual life too you can have a compass. There are also other ways of finding your way even if you cannot see where you are going. What do the occupants of a submarine do to navigate in the depths of the ocean? Nothing, but the submarine is equipped with devices giving out readings that the captain can interpret and so avoid incidents.

Well, human beings are like submarines insofar as, inwardly, they carry devices that allow them to find their way in the invisible world. These devices are their body and their subtle centres: energy centres like the aura, the solar plexus, the hara and the chakras. For the moment, however, these devices are covered in rust because they have not been used for incarnations, or they are broken because of the disordered life these human beings have led. So it is now up to them to put them back in working order through exercises and, no matter what happens, they will know clearly which direction they should head in.

2 August

*P*robably at least once in your life, you have had the sudden sensation of identifying with a man or a woman you are looking at or listening to, or with something you are contemplating in nature: a river, a waterfall, a spring, a star, the blue sky, the sun...

If we have this ability to identify with other beings, then in reality we are far more than we appear to be. As individuals we are X, Y, or Z, with a particular physical appearance, an identity, a name and so on. But in our soul and spirit we are the whole universe, we are everyone and everything. Literature holds many examples of this kind of experience, but many people consider it madness, or at best, poetic imagination. According to those who are supposedly 'normal', someone who claims to exist in the trees, the lakes, the mountains, the stars and the sun, or to have experienced himself as the deity, is obviously a poet or a madman. And yet, this poet or this madman describes the reality of every human being.

3 August

*P*eople often use the pretext of love to justify their behaviour to those they love. Once they say they 'love' someone, that is it; it never occurs to them to examine the nature of this love and their way of showing it. From the moment the feeling of love has befallen them, they have to succumb to it. Even reason is forsaken and the intellect is silenced. The intellect has no say in the matter once the heart has launched itself into love. If intellect tries to have its say, the heart replies, 'Be quiet. I'm talking, love is talking, and what do you have to add to that?'

The more a person has progressed on the path of evolution, the less they succumb to the demands of their feelings; they analyse whether they are disinterested, pure and useful, not only for others but also for themselves. But such people are rare. This is why there are so many novels, plays and films telling the comical and all-too-often disastrous stories of people who are in love. If human beings were able to make feeling and thought work together, love would manifest itself in far more beautiful forms and colours.

4 August

*F*or many believers, prayer is a matter of expressing their grievances to God. However, they should instead realize that the Creator has given them all the means, both physical and spiritual, to look after their needs and even those of others, and prayer should simply serve to help them rise within themselves to discover those means. One might say that God already did his part for us long ago. It is not for him to give humans what they lack, but for humans to search for it. What is the point of people praying to ask him for health or the affection of others if they continue to live in a way that makes them ill or disagreeable? And what good is it to pray for peace if, wherever they go, they continue to carry a veritable battlefield within them?

Prayer is, undoubtedly, an expression of faith, but faith must be understood as the force that incites human beings to surpass themselves, to transcend themselves. There are two kinds of faith: one is inspired by effort and activity, and the other is inspired by laziness, and this faith, which should rather be called naivety, is useless, and even harmful.

5 August

A very modest, simple person with a basic education can, through their inner searching, come to know more about life than the greatest scholars. It is for this reason that scientists should demonstrate a little more humility and reserve. God has not given them exclusive rights to knowledge. They can control matter, but they cannot control life, because life is not discovered by looking through a few instruments, lenses or microscopes, it is discovered deep within oneself.

Even someone who conducts investigations on stars and other planets can be as ignorant inwardly as if they had never left their cave. It is a matter of consciousness. What is the use, then, of setting out to discover the universe if we remain inwardly as limited as someone who has never stepped outside their remote village? The astronaut in his shuttle travels throughout space, but the shepherd who looks after his flock in the mountains and contemplates the starry sky in the silence of night perhaps knows more of immensity than the astronaut.

6 August

Women have much to reproach men for, because men have for centuries used and abused their physical superiority and their authority to force women to be in their service. Men have shown themselves to be careless, egocentric, unjust, violent and cruel. And now the situation has changed and women are gaining their independence. They are waking up and rising up. But if they get up to take revenge, the results will be no better, not even for them. Women must now show themselves generous and forgive men. Since they are the mothers, since their nature leads them to be good, tolerant, compassionate and ready to give love and to sacrifice themselves, they must not look to make men pay for everything men subjected them to.

Women must rise above their personal interests in order to awaken to higher virtues in the light. It is therefore up to all women on earth to come together, to join forces to work together and build: work on the children they bring into the world and on the men, the fathers of their children. This is how they will play their part in the regeneration of humankind.

7 August

Jesus said in the Gospels, *'And this is life eternal, that they may know You, the only true God.'* And how is it that we can *'know'* God? By merging with him. But this fusion can take place only between objects or beings of the same nature, the same essence.

For example, take a small amount of mercury, scatter it into droplets, then bring these droplets together, and once again they form only one drop. Now suppose that before gathering the droplets together, you allow a little dust to fall on some of them: however you try to reunite them, you will not succeed. Well, this is what happens to those who want to fuse with God but have not first purified themselves. While they remain impure, sombre and mean-spirited, they cannot unite with the Creator, who is beauty, light and love. All their impurities form a barrier which prevents this union. In order to rid themselves of these impurities, they must learn to master themselves, to control their thoughts and desires, and only then can they attune themselves to divine vibrations and waves and taste eternal life.

8 August

Imagine you have two bottles filled with perfume: as receptacles they are separate, but the fragrances that escape from them rise up do not remain separate for very long and they mix.

What is the purpose of this imagery? Well, human beings can be compared to bottles of perfume, in that their bodies are separate but with their thoughts and feelings they are able to meet with other human beings and even with entities from the invisible world. Only, we do not meet with anyone we want; we can only reach the souls and spirits in the visible and invisible worlds that correspond to what we ourselves are, because it is just a phenomenon of resonance that is at work here. The purpose, therefore, of prayer, meditation and all spiritual exercises is that they help us elevate our inner self and as we do so, by the power of affinity, we meet with ever purer and ever more luminous spirits.

9 August

*A*ll creatures living on earth – stones, plants, animals and human beings – receive life from the sun and from its warmth and light. But with their level of consciousness being higher than that of stones, plants and animals, human beings can do more than simply receiving this life passively. If they learn how to look at the sun and how to work with it, they will understand the nature of this energy it radiates and how they can capture and transform this energy by developing their subtle centres.

Initiates have learned to work with the purest quintessence of solar energy. For them it represents a food that they absorb and assimilate in order to project it around them. This is why they can then enlighten, warm and vivify other creatures. The true power of an initiate comes from their ability to transform light.

10 August

*H*ow many people complain, 'I seek the light. I pray every day, but God does not hear me. I have so many problems, I am unhappy and sick, and my life no longer has any meaning.' Whose fault is that? If people are struggling with so many problems, it means they have attracted them. They might say, 'Attracted? But how? This is not what I wanted, I did not know.' But yes, when you asked, you forgot certain laws. 'Ah but I did not know.' Maybe, but whether they knew or not, they have transgressed laws and are now suffering the consequences. Ignorance is never an excuse. If you do not respect the rules of the road, the police arrive and fine you, and it is useless to say, 'But, Officer, I did not know.' He calmly continues to write the ticket and does not want to hear whether you knew or not because, as far as he is concerned, you should have known.

From now on, therefore, try to bring your behaviour into greater harmony with your spiritual aspirations. You will no longer have the excuse of not knowing, and if you are negligent, you will be doubly guilty and will suffer.

11 August

*I*f you run away from certain work and effort that life imposes on you, you will never manage to make progress within. Some people can no longer stand their family or their work, and they leave. Others run away from their responsibilities. The fact is that running away is not recommended. Destiny puts you in certain situations for a reason.

You must strengthen yourself and face the difficulties and obstacles of your daily life. Consider sportsmen who train, climbers who test themselves against the mountain, and sailors who confront the ocean, braving bad weather and great dangers. Try to do as they do, not physically of course, because not everyone is prepared for such feats; but psychologically, train yourself to stand firm, to hold on. Of course, if a time comes when the situation becomes untenable, you must move on. But as soon as you can, come back and face things... until you become really steadfast and strong to complete your task.

12 August

Some people take on the role of spiritual guide without realising that they lack the necessary faculties and qualities of wisdom, love, disinterestedness, discernment and patience. They don't know how dangerous it is to shoulder this overwhelming task if they have not received heaven's approval.

To take on the responsibility of being a spiritual guide, you must first receive the qualification. Yes, we too receive qualifications in the spiritual world. The luminous spirits who sent us to earth observe and assess us, and if they see someone who has successfully passed the exams which life has imposed on them, they give them a diploma, which in turn gives them the right to teach. And where is this diploma? It is certainly not a piece of paper that can be destroyed: it is like a seal printed on a person's face and body, an integral part of the person themself, and it shows that they have been successful in working continuously on themself. Other human beings perhaps do not see it, but all the spirits of nature, all the spirits of light see it from afar, and they hasten to help them with their task.

13 August

*T*he feeling of loneliness is one of the most terrible forms of suffering that human beings can experience. Each of us needs to find someone with whom we can share our thoughts, feelings, and aspirations, someone with whom we can exchange harmoniously every day. This ideal being is obviously very difficult to find, and many books have explained the pain, anguish and feeling of abandonment experienced by men and women when they are unable to find what some have called their soul mate!

But, in reality, the human soul can only be filled permanently and completely by God. If you wish to feel that you are not alone every day, that you are surrounded by beings who love and understand you, and that you yourself are filled with a great presence of joy and light, you must unite with God and his manifestations, which are wisdom, love and truth. For God himself is love, wisdom and truth. And for the person who places love in their heart, wisdom in their head, and truth in their will, solitude no longer exists.

Not only does pleasure not bring happiness, it is often the pursuit of pleasure that stops you from finding happiness. Pleasure is an enjoyable and fleeting sensation that leads human beings to believe that by making it last as long as possible, they will be happy. Well, no. Why? Because the experiences that quickly and easily give them an enjoyable sensation do not, for the most part, exist in the higher planes. They affect only the physical body, maybe the heart and barely the intellect. But we cannot be happy if we seek to satisfy solely the physical body, the heart or even the intellect, because such satisfaction is limited and short-lived.

Unlike pleasure, true happiness is not a sensation of the moment and it affects the entire being: soul and spirit. So, when you find someone or something appealing or pleasant, do not rush. Use these criteria and ask yourself whether it is really here that you will find happiness.

15 August

Review all that you have accepted up to now in the form of knowledge, ideas and opinions; study them and ask yourselves whether they are consistent with the initiatic philosophy you follow. If they do, emphasize them, reinforce them and reflect more deeply on them. But for notions that go against this philosophy, be aware that they will lead you astray and create problems for you. So reject them. This might seem difficult or impossible at first, but you will then feel so much freer and lighter, and you will see so much more clearly!

If, for the time being, you are still floundering in the dark, if you still feel hesitant, indecisive or constrained, it is because you are burdened with too many things which weigh you down and obscure your sight. It is time to sort through things. Go within and try to identify what you need throw away and what you must keep: you will feel lighter and become more clear-sighted.

16 August

*H*ow have revolutions taken place in the past? Did all participants have to be politicians, lawyers, philosophers, scientists or generals? No, but all were present and united – scientists, the ignorant, the competent and incompetent, the weak and the strong – and together they emerged victorious! Every day we see this type of event reported in books, in newspapers, on the radio or on television, but we do not understand. You might say, 'But what is there to understand?' Many things, and in particular, that to obtain results, it is the numbers of people uniting together that counts. Whether the individuals in the crowd be drunkards or invalids is of secondary importance. The important thing is that, drunkards and invalids though they may be, they join with all the others in their claim for change.

And in order to claim the kingdom of God, what is important? Of course, everyone must make an effort to mature within, and to move forward on the path of good. But, above all, they must all stand together in order for their claim to be heard at last.

17 August

*F*rom disorder to order, from chaos to harmony, such is the law of creation, and everywhere in the universe we can observe this law at work. Yes, we see it everywhere, except in what our contemporaries insist on calling art, which is more often, in fact, only a return to the formless. We look at a painting or a piece of sculpture without being able to distinguish what it represents. Inarticulate sounds pass for a song, cacophony and noise pass for music, words thrown together pass for poetry, and disorganised movements pass for dance...

The intelligence of living nature always works in the direction of differentiation and organisation: a single cell divides and multiplies, and a few months later a human being or an animal appears, extraordinary in form. Must we now take the opposite path and become unicellular, or chaotic? How is it that artists, who are by definition creators, have not understood the law their creations must obey?

18 August

*H*uman beings do not understand where their rejection of certain laws will lead because they have never studied the far-reaching consequences of a thought, a word or an action. If they had more discernment, they would sense that at the exact moment they reject these laws, they become weaker, because they open the door to dark powers which seize them and bind them hand and foot. It is a law: the less we control our thoughts, our desires, and our whims, the more enslaved we become.

You may say that you want to be free to satisfy your desires. Fine, but you must know that this is the direct path to slavery. You will be a slave to yourself, or rather to very primitive inner forces which will strike you down and take complete control over you. True freedom begins with mastery of oneself. When wise men advise human beings to learn to master their impulses, it is not for the pleasure of bullying them, but because they know that the absence of mastery opens the way to illness, imbalance, and death.

19 August

'*Praise be to God*'... To understand what these words mean, it would be better for those who read or hear them to be less obsessed by human glories. So many naive and ignorant people think God is like one of many tyrannical and vain monarchs who expect people to worship their wealth, their qualities and their achievements and who are only satisfied if they appear greater than all those around them. God has no need for us to sing his praises, for nothing we might say of him could add anything to him. The entire universe and all the angelic hierarchies already sing his praise. Rather it is we who need to glorify him, so that we may enter into His light.

And to glorify God, it is not enough to repeat endlessly that he is great, powerful and wise either. It is through our efforts to purify our thoughts, our feelings, our desires and our actions that we glorify God. In doing so we will enter into the light of divine glory and, wherever a ray of this light falls, we too will be present.

20 August

*S*o many people are devastated because they feel they have been betrayed. They exclaim repeatedly, 'But how is it possible? He promised me... She gave me her word...' It is true, they were promised a great deal, that they would not be abandoned, that they would always be loved, helped and supported and they believed what they were told. But they should not have been so gullible! Most men and women, like children, make promises that they genuinely believe they can keep. When they give their word they are sincere and are convinced they will do what they say. But they do not know themselves, they do not know how weak, unstable and fickle they are and, when the time comes, they lose their nerve or forget. This is normal, and you must know in advance that this is always possible. If you never want to be disappointed, try to be sensible. Never ask human beings to do something that may be beyond their capacity because, even with the best intentions in the world, they may not be able to live up to your expectations.

21 August

When the sun is hidden by clouds, it does not disappear; it continues to spread its light and warmth. When the clouds eventually disperse, or if we are able to rise high enough in the atmosphere, we see that the sun is always there. Well, an identical phenomenon often takes place within us.

Like the sun, God is always there, present and unchanging, sending us his light (his wisdom) and his warmth (his love) to all beings. But if we allow clouds to form within us by means of thoughts, feelings and desires that are chaotic, selfish and negative, we will allow clouds to form within and be deprived of this light and warmth. Instead of complaining that God does not exist, or that he has abandoned us, human beings must understand that if they find themselves in the dark and the cold, they alone are responsible for their situation and must do all they can to rise above the clouds.

22 *August*

Why belong to a spiritual brotherhood? There are many reasons; one of them being that a spiritual community gives its members the best conditions in which to transform themselves and to advance. Even if they wish to improve themselves, those who remain alone do not always have the will to continue their efforts: for a short while they do their exercises, but then they give up and no one knows when they will start again... and give up once more. It is easier in a community because they are stimulated and supported.

Yes, by virtue of example, those around us have an enormous influence on us. So many people, whether through debauchery, alcohol, drugs or crime, have done things which they would never have done on their own! If we admit that a group has the power to lead people into wrong-doing, why not accept that it can be equally powerful in leading them towards good?

23 August

*T*hese days people are increasingly convinced that exposing themselves to nature and the four elements (earth, water, air and sunshine) benefits their health. They do so in various states of undress, but this is not really the point. 'Then what is the point?' you might ask. The point is that what they receive will depend above all on their thoughts and feelings.

The skin itself is neutral, and is capable of allowing everything to pass through it, both good and bad. What directs and determines the work of the skin is our consciousness. According to what is in your mind and heart, the skin can favour or prevent certain elements passing through. If your thoughts and feelings are pure, luminous and filled with respect and love for nature and its many forces, it is as if your skin received an order from above to drive out poisons and to attract only life-giving particles and energies. If carried out under the right conditions, this communion with the four elements can purify you both physically and spiritually.

24 August

*S*ome people claim they cannot listen to music, that they do not understand it. But what does this mean? It is not comprehension that counts in music, but the sensations you experience as a result of its vibrations, of the musical harmony. Do we understand birdsong, the murmuring of springs or streams, or the rustling of the wind in the branches? No, but we are captivated and filled with wonder, and it is this which is essential.

For the same reasons, it is always better to sing songs in their original language, even if we do not understand their meaning at first. There is a relationship between the words and music, which is destroyed in translation. Music is not created to be understood, but to be felt. Even when it is accompanied by words, the meaning of these words is of less importance than their sound. So study carefully the states which music evokes in you, and use them for your spiritual work.

25 August

*A*t one time or another you have met a man or a woman who has inspired in you a deep feeling of affection. Did you notice the transformations that this feeling alone produced within you? Suddenly you began to think and behave differently, not only towards this person, but with everyone around you. Even your relationship with nature and objects changed. So many things that you did not see or feel before begin to reveal themselves to you, encouraging you to pursue other interests! Because love is a force and this force acts on you, it influences your mind, your will, and even your body and it opens up great possibilities for you.

Love is like the fuel in your car: if your tank is full, you can go a long way, but if it is empty, how far can you go? And if love is missing, where can you go?

26 August

*S*o many murky layers lie between our ordinary consciousness and our divine consciousness! This is why our most important work is to apply the methods that will enable us to break up the deposits within us, the slag which blocks the manifestation of wisdom, strength and divine love within us.

The alchemists of the past sought the universal solvent to prepare the philosopher's stone. But a true alchemist seeks to dissolve the dark matter within them, the negative instigator and dangerous conductor which blocks our union with God. And do you want to know what the best solvent is? Humility. But this solvent acts effectively only if we know why and how we must be humble; it does not mean we must indiscriminately belittle and disparage ourselves. When it is misunderstood, humility can cause as much harm as pride. True humility enables us to dissolve our lower nature in order to identify with the divine.

27 *August*

There are children who have never known their parents, who do not even know who they are, but they never doubt that they had a father and a mother. In fact, many spend their lives hoping to find them and looking for the slightest clue to their existence. The truth is that their parents, whose absence makes them suffer so, are in fact within them: in all that they have bequeathed to them as physical and psychic traits. Therefore, whether they are physically present or not, what is essential is always present within: children always have their parents with them, within them.

Biologists and psychologists study children to see how the laws of heredity apply to them. This is important, but it is not enough. Who will now study our divine heritage, all those divine seeds received from our heavenly Father and Mother, which we must develop a little more in order to resemble them?

28 August

When students pass their exams, they receive a diploma that opens certain doors for them: they can continue their studies, find a job, and so on. In the same way, when we pass the tests of life successfully, we receive a diploma which gives us more opportunities and confidence to keep advancing.

You might ask, 'But what is this diploma?' It is not a piece of paper like the university diplomas that can be lost or destroyed. This diploma is like a mark which the invisible world applies to our face, to our whole body, and it is imprinted so deeply within us that nothing and no-one can take it away. And then, even the spirits of the four elements, who know how to read this diploma, recognise us. Wherever we go, they see this diploma, and it is a signal to them that they must welcome us, protect us, and help us.

29 August

Meditation is breathing, so too is prayer, ecstasy and all communication with heaven. Those who wish to deepen the meaning of the process of breathing can gradually feel their own breathing merge into the breathing of God. For God too breathes: he breathes out and a world appears, he breathes in and a world disappears... We can get a small glimpse of this process on certain days in summer when we see light white clouds suddenly appear in the sky, and a moment later they just as suddenly disappear...

God's in-breaths and out-breaths obviously take place over billions and billions of years. The sacred books of India tell us that one day God will breathe in and our universe will return within him. And then, again, he will breathe out and a new creation will appear... Through human beings, God breathes more quickly, but in the cosmos, his breathing is a lot slower. And therefore, the slower our breathing, the closer we come to divine breathing.

30 August

Someone who feels betrayed by a person in whom they had put their faith tends to react negatively. Because they suffer the unfaithful, dishonest behaviour of others, they consider them as an enemy and seek a means for revenge. But they don't know that reacting in this way will do even more harm.

Imagine you did not know you should have confidence in someone who deserved it: this is an error of judgement and yes, you will suffer some consequences. But if you adopt a hostile attitude, the damage you suffer will be much more serious. For not only do negative sentiments and the desire for revenge disturb your inner harmony, but you will also lose this person forever. Yes, they have behaved badly, but if you yourself know how to act, if you give them the chance to realize and rectify their mistake, with time they will perhaps become a true friend again.

31 August

Anyone who strives in their inner life to give priority to the activity of the spirit, their higher self, is already participating in the cosmic work of Christ, of God himself. Yes, this activity which takes place in another sphere, most often without our knowledge, is something mysterious, but is a reality.

When you are absorbed in your daily tasks, you cannot begin to imagine what your higher self is doing. One day, perhaps, when your mind is sufficiently developed, you will become conscious of the work it carries out in all regions of the universe. For the time being, it is essential to become aware of its presence within you. How? First of all, during your meditations, start by making peace with the inhabitants within you and put them in the service of love and light. Gradually this work will take place naturally, without your having to think about it, and because of it you will reunite with your higher self which is a quintessence of God himself.

1 September

*F*or centuries thinkers have said that humanity is like a body, and that the countries of the world are its organs. But in truth, very few people have been working to inspire the organs of humanity with the same wisdom and disinterestedness as the organs of the physical body; everyone thinks only of themselves, to the detriment of their neighbour. It is time therefore to take the example of the human organism that nature has so skilfully designed and to study how it functions, when it is in good or ill health, and to understand that the same rules apply to the whole of humanity.

When the brain is lucid and the heart dilated, even the feet feel well. Yes, when an organ is in good health, all the other parts of the body feel it and rejoice; and when an organ is deficient, the others, poor things, feel undermined as well. So why, when a country is in difficulty, do its neighbours rejoice? This proves that they are unhealthy organs, and do not realize that sooner or later they too will suffer the consequences.

2 September

*T*he universe is a kind of sanctuary for us which we must approach with a sense of the sacred. For not only is nature alive, it is also intelligent. And if we open ourselves to it, it responds by allowing us to participate in its life. You may think that all natural phenomena happen mechanically and that there is therefore no intelligence involved. Well, you are mistaken. Human beings have observed that the universe obeys laws, and this has made it possible for them to create what they call 'the natural sciences', but this is no reason to conclude that natural phenomena are purely 'mechanical'. In thinking this way, you denigrate both nature and yourself; you make it impossible for life to pour into your heart, into your soul, into your mind, and even into your physical body.

You will become truly alive only when you decide to enter into relationship with this great and endless life present everywhere in the universe.

3 September

*P*erhaps you have never travelled in a hot-air balloon, but you know that what enables it to rise in the sky is the heat produced by the combustion of a gas, which inflates the canvas and makes the balloon lighter than air. The same is true in the spiritual life: to rise higher we must become light and dilated and, in order to become dilated, we must heat something within us. It is the warmth of love that inflates the heart and renders it so light that it begins to rise like a balloon.

You see, in order to move closer to heaven, it is more useful to know how to read the book of nature than the books of the theologians. The book of nature teaches you that when you become cold, you contract and become heavy, heavier than air, and you fall. And when you find yourself on the ground, you of course complain that heaven has abandoned you. But warm your heart, fill it with love, and you will rise once again and travel in space.

4 September

No matter how enthusiastic you are about the religion or spiritual teaching you have discovered, do not begin by preaching it to others. First of all, people have heard enough sermons on the subject, and it is your actions alone that will convince them. Secondly, to do so is not good for you either.

A spiritual conviction must be lived in the depths of your being so that it becomes a part of you. If you begin preaching to everyone, something within you will begin to disintegrate, and the slightest jolt will throw you off balance. Even if you remain faithful to the principles, they will rapidly lose their vibrancy; and you will become hardened and parched, because the spring within you will have run dry. You must find very subtle ways to express your convictions. Otherwise you will lose them or, even worse, they will soon turn to fanaticism.

5 September

*A*t one time or another in your life you will be the victim of injustice, of false accusations, and mistaken judgments by people who want to harm and destroy you. It is important to know this and to prepare yourself for such situations so that, when the time comes, you will not allow anxiety, grief or the desire for revenge to get the upper hand. The only correct response in these situations is to continue to work on yourself. Tell yourself that everything inspired by the divine world will endure and will shine one day in all its glory, whereas self-interest, intrigue and scheming, although they may succeed for a certain time, will sooner or later fail.

Therefore, leave those who are unjust and spiteful to get stuck in their swamps, if that is what they want; they will become weak and impoverished because they do not know how terrible the laws are for those who serve jealousy, deceit and hatred. The power of heaven is infinite: it works imperceptibly but tirelessly, and everything eventually ends well for those who hold in their lives a sublime ideal of beauty and love: the coming of the kingdom of God and brotherhood in the world.

6 September

Life is merely a series of exchanges between our inner and outer worlds, but we must always give priority to the inner world, because it is with this that we are continually connected. Yes, you are not always looking at, listening to, touching or tasting something outside yourself, but you are always with yourself, with your thoughts, your feelings and your states of consciousness. Therefore, as long as you favour the outer world over the inner world, you run the risk of being deeply disappointed. For a moment, perhaps, you have the illusion of holding onto something, but a while later you hold nothing, because everything has eluded you.

Human beings seek something to fulfil them, something they are not always able to define, even though they call it happiness. They must know that it is first within them – by organising their inner world – that they will come to find this happiness.

7 September

A spiritual master is a being who possesses great psychic powers, but these powers do not allow him to act at all times, in every location, under any circumstances, and with just anyone.

A verse of the Gospels says that, when passing through Nazareth, Jesus did not perform many miracles because of the scepticism of its inhabitants. So, even though he possessed great powers, he did not reveal them before people who were not open or trusting. And to the man who requested healing for himself or for his child, he replied, *'According to your faith, may it be to you'*, or, *'Your faith has made you well'*. Of course, those who are ignorant will say that Jesus was self-centred and vain, and this is why he agreed to help only those who had blind faith in him. No, the true explanation is that faith and doubt can be compared to chemical compounds: faith is made of subtle elements which favour fulfilment, and doubt is made of elements that oppose it.

8 September

*B*oth noise and silence are languages. Silence can express the end of movement, the absence of life, but it is also the language of perfection. While noise is the expression of life, but this life is often disordered and needs to be mastered and developed. For example, children are noisy because they are overflowing with energy and vitality. On the contrary, old people are silent. This is partly because their energy has diminished and because noise tires them, but it is also often due to the fact that they have evolved, that they have gone deeper into themselves, and that it is their spirit which encourages them to be silent. In order to review their life, to reflect on it and to draw lessons from it, they need this silence in which a work of detachment, simplification and synthesis can be carried out.

The pursuit of silence is an inner process which leads human beings towards the light and a true understanding of things.

9 September

*I*t is in thinking about others and working for them that we become wealthy. At first of course, the exact opposite is true. In the beginning, those who are full of love, kindness, and self-sacrifice are considered a little foolish and are used and abused by those around them. But as time passes, they are appreciated more and more, and one day everyone expresses their love for them. They just need to be patient.

When you put a sum of money in the bank, you do not receive the interest right away, do you? You must wait. Exactly the same law applies in the spiritual realm. You work with a great deal of love and disinterestedness, and at first you see no results. But you must not be discouraged: one day wealth will come to you from every direction, and you will not be able to escape it even if you try. The entire universe will shower you with extraordinary riches, because it is you who have engendered them. This is one of the forms of justice.

10 September

*I*n order to understand what true religion is, human beings must draw closer to the light, warmth and life of the sun. That is to say, they must seek the wisdom which enlightens them and resolves all problems, the disinterested love which beautifies, encourages and consoles them, and the subtle, spiritual life which renders them active, dynamic and daring, so that they may create the kingdom of God and his justice on earth. And no one can destroy this religion: anyone who tries to combat it will only weaken and disfigure themselves.

When this understanding of a universal religion penetrates every mind, the whole organisation of life will become universal: there will be no more separation between human beings, no more borders or wars. As they come to know the sun in its sublime expression of light, warmth and life, human beings will draw closer and closer to the divine, and they will transform the earth into a garden of paradise where all will live as brothers and sisters. Everyone must accept this universal religion which the sun teaches us.

11 September

You might say, 'I am free to do what I want and the others will just have to accept me as I am.' Well, go ahead: you will push people around, put your feet on the table, push aside those who bother you, indulge in all sorts of excesses, and you will be very proud of yourself... But one day you will be cornered, because an act is never without consequences. 'What do you mean "cornered"? Why would I be cornered?' Because under the pretext of asserting your power, consciously or unconsciously, you constantly transgress human laws, but also – and this is more serious – divine laws. This means that you will be preparing very bad conditions in your head, heart and body. And this is how you will be cornered one day.

To convince themselves that they are strong, independent and free, people embark on dangerous paths. They fail to understand that their continuing transgressions represent a corresponding number of debts to be paid; and gradually they give way beneath that great weight.

12 September

*I*t is one thing to know the laws of destiny and to understand that nothing that happens to human beings – happy or unhappy – is by chance, and it is another thing to find the attitude that best allows us to help them. Some might say, 'But if they must go through hardships which are imposed on them by certain laws, why try helping them?' No, it is not right to draw such categorical conclusions.

In truth, the efforts we make to help others are never wasted: in some circumstances, the lords of destiny can be swayed in their favour, having noticed your love and good will. And these efforts are also useful for you: they help you progress. In helping others, your thoughts, feelings, and generous actions also have a positive effect on you yourself. So, help others, and you will be the first to feel better!

13 September

*T*eenagers, who do not know much about the mechanisms of the psychic life, do not suspect the danger of letting their imagination run out of control. And it seems also that parents and teachers, who did the same in their youth, let young people immerse themselves in nebulous states, and even sometimes encourage them by saying, 'He's dreaming, he's a poet, we must let him dream.' But what do they know about this world of daydreams? In reality, it is the astral world with all its seductions, illusions and snares.

One of the wonderful powers nature has put into human beings is imagination, but it becomes dangerous if it is not mastered. If young people – adults too – let just any feeling, any desire gain a hold over their imagination, they will eventually fall a prey to currents and dark entities which will seriously trouble their mind. Imagination must always be oriented in a positive and constructive direction, towards the world of light symbolised by the sun.

14 September

Not only do human beings believe they have nothing to lose by cutting themselves off from universal harmony, but they are convinced that by detaching themselves from the laws of nature and struggling against them, they will gain freedom and become powerful. Well, this is the greatest mistake.

Human beings become truly powerful and free only when they learn to vibrate in harmony with the universe, when they are able to hear the symphony of all nature in which everything sings: the forests, the rivers and the stars. It is this cosmic symphony that we call the music of the spheres. And in order to hear the music of the spheres, we must begin by harmonizing our entire being, all our organs, all the cells of our organs, by unremitting and profound work. The moment the very smallest particles of our being vibrate in unison, the symphony of the universe will be revealed to us.

15 September

Why is believing in God so obvious to some people and to others an illusion or an absurdity? The explanation is simple: at birth each human being comes to earth with the sum of experiences they have lived in their previous incarnations. If someone spontaneously has faith, it is because what they have studied and verified in their previous lives is recorded in their soul and manifests in this life as an intuition of the divine world. If they now recognise the existence of their heavenly Father, it is because they have been with him for a long time. They have communed with him and have been left with such powerful imprints that they cannot doubt: they know. Faith is therefore knowledge based on experience.

Those who have experimented in the lower regions of their being in previous incarnations draw conclusions from those experiences which they think are the truth. And those who have experimented in the higher realms of the soul and spirit also draw conclusions, and they can no longer have any doubts that a higher intelligence manifests itself in the world.

16 September

Sometimes people ask my advice about their choice of profession. They are hesitant: should they commit themselves to a certain line of work which would earn them a good deal of money, or should they choose a job which is less lucrative but which would leave them free for altruistic activities? As a teacher, it is not my place to tell others that they should do this or that, but only to explain the consequences of their choices, and it is then up to them to decide.

So my response is as follows. There is nothing wrong with choosing an occupation where you will earn a great deal of money, but it all depends on what you want to achieve. If your ideal is, as they say, 'to be successful in life', which means to live a life of ease, to have power and influence, so then, go and earn a lot of money! But if your ideal is to deepen your inner life, you don't really need money, but instead you need freedom: that is free time of course, but above all freedom of spirit. In this way, you will be able to concentrate of the activities where you will be free from the constraints imposed by materialistic life.

17 September

*B*ecause life is a succession of efforts, suffering, and obstacles to overcome, human beings are obliged to struggle, and in struggling they become weak and exhausted. You can see this happening: day by day, something within them dulls and disintegrates. Why? Because they did not know how to connect with the ever-flowing, inexhaustible source, the only one that can give them water that is ever fresh, life that is ever new.

To be alive is to be able to renew and regenerate oneself, but those who truly know what it means to renew oneself are rare. Most people confuse what is new with what is different. No, change does not necessarily bring about something that is really new. Only that which comes from the divine source is new, truly new, and we must connect with this source in order to regenerate ourselves.

18 September

*E*verything is alive, everything vibrates and radiates. If you were clairvoyant you would see this radiance throughout creation. But even if you do not see it, you can feel it, which is even more important because, where the inner life, the spiritual life is concerned, feeling is superior to seeing.

It is possible to see and yet to feel nothing. What most human beings do is proof of this: they see, but they do not benefit much from what they see, because they are imprisoned deep inside themselves, with the doors and windows firmly locked; almost nothing reaches their conscience and sensitivity. And if God himself were to come and visit, no doubt they would look at him with a critical eye, because they would not like many things about him. So, seeing in itself changes nothing deep within; it is feeling that gives us the best understanding of reality.

19 September

*I*f a person has no faith in good, they risk losing whatever qualities or faculties they possess. Why? Because without faith in good, the best qualities and faculties have no solid foundations and all kinds of consequences automatically arise: their thought processes and way of seeing things become distorted. They endlessly view people and situations with suspicion, and are afraid. Fear, of course, is a very bad counsellor. How many people in the grip of fear are guilty of cowardice, injustice and spitefulness! Despite all their good qualities, they allow themselves to be invaded by this irrational and uncontrollable instinct. And when the fear has passed, they are often ashamed of what they have done, but by then it is too late.

In order to conquer fear, we must believe steadfastly in the power of good, which is to say, in the pre-eminence of the spirit in you.

20 September

*B*reathing and its workings have been studied closely by yogis in India for many thousands of years and they have understood their importance for our vitality and also for the correct functioning of our mind. And since they researched the subject so thoroughly, they also discovered that all the rhythms in our body are related to cosmic rhythms. So, in order to make contact with certain entities or regions in the spiritual world, we need to find its specific rhythm and use it as we would a key.

This is exactly what happens when we seek to tune into a radio programme on a specific frequency. In order to receive the frequency emitted by a particular station, we need to know its specific wavelength. The same goes for breathing: in order to make contact with a specific region in the universe, we must know which rhythm to use.

21 September

*E*ven if those who preach Christianity strive to remember the precept given by Jesus, *'Love your enemies'*, in reality there are very few people capable of applying it. The majority do not even know how to love their friends, so how can they love their enemies? It is so difficult! In order to succeed in applying this selfless and impersonal conception of love, we must connect with a being who manifests this commandment fully: the sun. Watch, and you will see that however human beings behave, the sun continues to send them its light and warmth, to nourish and vivify them.

If you want to understand the highest moral code, you will find it in the sun, and only there. And since the sun represents the spirit within you, when looking at it, force yourself to rise to those regions within you where you feel that nothing can touch you. Because it is only from here that, whatever happens to you, you can continue to send out your light and your love.

22 September

Get into the habit of observing and listening to the life of nature: to stones, plants, animals, but also to the four elements – earth, water, air, fire – and the different forms in which they appear: rocks, sand, rain, snow, wind, clouds, sun, stars and so on. There are so many things to study and interpret!

Just look at the shape, colours and density of clouds: sometimes they appear like cavalcades, battles, feasts... It is the spirits of the air, beings we call sylphs or elves, at work. There is quite a life up above, which expresses itself through a vast number of shapes: faces, birds, flocks of sheep, landscapes... There is even writing we still do not know how to decipher. But it does not matter, the essential thing is to let oneself be impregnated consciously by all these images, for this is how we make contact with the life of nature.

23 September

*E*very judgement human beings hold about people and things depends on a comparison: they prefer one person to another, or one thing to another. In order to prefer something, to judge, people must have made a comparison in one way or another. They spend their lives comparing their houses and their cars to those of their neighbours. They strive to keep up with those who have more things, better things, and more beautiful things, because they believe them to be happier.

In the material realm, human beings are experts at making comparisons, but they are less inclined to make them in the spiritual realm. If they meet a sage, someone who is disinterested, full of love and a master of himself, they do not ask themselves, 'But how do I measure up next to him?' Well, with this mentality, it is impossible to advance. In order to progress, they must compare themselves to exceptional beings, to all the great spiritual masters of humanity, and say, 'How can I reconcile my understanding with theirs? Let me see if they can teach me a better way of thinking and behaving.'

24 September

*H*uman beings have still not resolved the problems of life as a community. Outwardly they may have formed nations and organised societies whose members support each other, and where everyone serves the whole and benefits from it. Inwardly, however, they remain isolated, aggressive and hostile towards one another. They have not learned how to apply all the progress they have made in their material and practical life – in the realm of organisation and technology – to their inner lives. That is why, despite all this progress, humanity is still suffering from the same misfortunes: wars, poverty, famine and oppression, on a scale unheard of until now.

Real improvements can take place only as a result of a profound change in mentality. Human beings must feel themselves connected to one another psychically and spiritually, in order to succeed in forming the only true society: a universal brotherhood. It is when every individual strives to attain the higher consciousness of unity that societies, peoples and nations will begin to live in peace and freedom.

25 September

You meet a person who you think is wonderful, you feel attracted to them, and you would like to become closer to them. Well, you must be prudent. Instead of trying at all cost to get as close as possible to them on the physical plane, learn to listen to the vibrations of their voice, to capture the light in their face and to rejoice in the harmony of their gestures. In this way, you will gradually succeed in relating to what is most subtle and spiritual in them, and you will taste new and indescribable sensations.

By adopting this attitude, you will finally discover that the men and women you have tended to look down on or ignore because of their modest and unimpressive appearance are, in fact, exceptional beings who will offer you much more than others who seem more interesting and more seductive.

26 September

*H*ow many opportunities are we given to transcend the mediocrity of daily life! But do you bother to pay attention to these occasions? The silence of the night, the starry sky, and the immensity of space offer us the best conditions for distancing ourselves a little from human affairs, for reflecting on other worlds where spiritual entities live in harmony and splendour. Nothing about our preoccupations, our worries and fears means anything to them; they are insignificant events. You might say, 'But what do you mean, insignificant events? Famine, wars, and murders are terrible!' Yes, they are terrible, but Cosmic Intelligence does not view them in the same way as we do.

For Cosmic Intelligence, only the events of the soul and the spirit are important. If human beings attached more importance to those events which could take place in their soul and their spirit, instead of giving priority to material affairs, they would be more selfless, more understanding and more open to others; and so much misery and tragedy could be avoided on earth.

27 September

You are all seeking this love of the so-called soul mate. Well, if you want to find your soul mate, above all, do not look for them. Concern yourself only with living a pure, intense, and luminous life. Simply live this life and let it take its course; it is this that will attract your soul mate to you. You do not yet know what such a life can do to bring you the beings who have an affinity with you. One day you will say, 'I did not seek my soul mate, I did not go searching for my beloved, and yet they came...from the far reaches of the universe.'

To find this soul mate, many people put advertisements in the papers and go to all kinds of receptions and night-clubs, but what do they find? Is it so difficult to understand that it is by nourishing something vital and luminous within ourselves every day that we eventually attract this marvellous being we hope for?

28 September

When you feel distressed and tormented it is simply because you have become lost in the psychic regions infested with lower entities – the enemies of humanity. And these entities attack you, and if you try to fight back to make them let go, since these entities are stronger than you, they have the upper hand. So what can you do?

A bird pecks at some grain on the ground, and a cat comes along. The bird does not wait to confront the cat, it flies away. But human beings have still not realized what birds have understood: they stay where they are to fight, and are stripped and destroyed. You might say, 'How can we fly away?' There are so many ways to do it! Through will-power, prayer, imagination, the memory of a light-filled moment, the wonder of nature... and all the works of art and literature. You have so many possibilities at your disposal! But do you really want to free yourself from this situation? No, you stay there without doing anything, except filling yourself up with pills and bothering other people by relating your distress and nightmares. From now on, try to put an end these negative states of mind by learning how to take wing.

29 September

When a certain number of people come together around an idea, their thoughts and desires alone create a living reality. This is a law of the spiritual world. And even if this reality is not made up of particles that are sufficiently material to be seen or touched, it exists, and we call this collective entity an egregor. An egregor is a living and active entity, and each country, each religion, and each philosophical movement has one.

The Universal White Brotherhood also has its egregor, and all its members, the brothers and sisters who gather together with the same ideal of peace and light, never stop nourishing and strengthening it. Not only can it then have a positive influence on other egregors in the world but, most of all, it contributes to the evolution of those who have worked to create it.

30 September

Kindness has a great deal to do with the will. Those who are kind are always motivated to show their thoughts and feelings through their actions. They devote themselves to supporting others: they come to their aid and at times even shake them or drag them away from their difficulties. Sometimes a gruff appearance hides a very kind heart.

But while kindness manifests itself by means of actions, it is something more than this. It requires several incarnations for human beings to truly succeed in developing this virtue which, in fact, represents one of the highest forms of intelligence. It is often said that those who are kind are a little stupid, but what a mistake! Those who devote their minds, their time and their energies to helping others are the most intelligent. To forget oneself in order to serve others is true intelligence.

1 October

*I*n itself, the need for change is not a bad thing, but in certain aspects of life, it can be detrimental to your development. In terms of a friendly or amorous relationship, it is best to hesitate in the beginning in order to weigh the pros and cons, but once you are committed, try not to back out. In the same way, before you commit yourself to a spiritual teaching and begin to follow a master, start by studying the situation carefully: ask yourself if this master is suited to your mentality, to your aspirations, to your ideal, and whether his teaching corresponds to your deeper nature. Once you have engaged yourself, it is best to keep up this commitment. What can you hope to build inwardly that is solid and stable by going first one way and then another, according to the impulses of your whims and your curiosity?

Spiritual experience does not comprise a series of meetings that one arranges first with a Hindu master, then with a Sufi master, then with a Zen master, and so on. Spiritual experience is a furrow that we plough within ourselves and that we must forever deepen.

2 October

*E*very day we meet different people and we cannot stop ourselves from spontaneously feeling either like or dislike for them, for these are natural feelings that even the sages experience. However, the difference between the sage and ordinary men and women is that the sage controls his dislikes and does not give way blindly to his likes, because he knows that neither one nor the other are good criteria.

Liking and disliking are often instinctive, purely personal feelings which originate in experiences lived in other lives. They do not provide impartial information about the value of a person, their qualities or their faults. Many imagine that their intuition dictates these reactions. No, not at all. That is why we must make a habit not only of behaving with understanding and kindness toward people we do not like, but also of recognising the mistakes and weaknesses of those we do like.

3 October

*H*aving heard of the laws of karma, some people become indifferent in the face of other people's suffering. If they see a good and honest person suffer they say to themselves that their suffering must be due to a past incarnation where they made mistakes that they now have to repair, and so they do nothing to help them. But perhaps they are wrong... When such people see others suffer, they always think it is justified, but when they themselves suffer, they feel that they do not deserve such injustice.

So what is the right attitude to have? Exactly the opposite: when you are suffering, tell yourself this suffering is most probably justified; but when others are suffering, tell yourself they are not guilty and try to understand and help them. This way of doing things will help your evolution greatly.

4 October

When you eat, you should make the habit of chewing food for a while so that the salivary glands have time to do their work, for saliva contains various chemical substances that participate in digestion. Their action can be compared to a kind of cooking that makes the assimilation of food easier. So, if we masticate food until it liquefies, only a small amount of waste is left over, and we benefit from a lot of energies, even by eating a little.

The same laws govern respiration. That is why, when you breathe, absorb air slowly and deeply, since it has to go down to the base of your lungs in order to expand them. And after inhaling, you have to retain it as if you were chewing it. The lungs could be said to masticate air, just as the mouth chews food. The air you inhale is like a 'mouthful' of food filled with energy and, in order to digest it well, you must exhale very slowly.

5 October

*T*o the rich young man who came to ask what rites he should observe in order to have eternal life, Jesus replied, *'Go, sell what you own, and give the money to the poor, then come, follow me.'* And the young man went away feeling sad, for what Jesus asked of him was beyond him. Must we conclude then that, in order to follow Jesus, we must truly rid ourselves of all we possess and give it to the poor? Some have done this, but not all have become better disciples as a result.

It is commendable to make sacrifices and renunciations, but what should we renounce and what should we sacrifice? We must strive to clarify our ideas on this subject. Material things weigh us down and obscure our view, but it is useless to renounce them if we do not at the same time rid ourselves of the thoughts, feelings and desires that encumber us even further and cloud our inner view.

6 October

*O*ne day someone was telling me about their difficulties with a friend: following a misunderstanding, their relations had deteriorated, and the hostile attitude of their friend hurt them deeply. My visitor explained to me, 'I really wish things would work themselves out. Every day I pray, I concentrate deeply, and I ask God to help me. But I see no improvement.'

I listened for a moment, and then I said, 'All that activity is magnificent! But why call on all the heavenly powers to help with a tiny problem that you can solve yourself? A look, a few words and a selfless gesture would no doubt be all it takes for your friend to understand that you are still their friend. You ask God to intervene – and that is a very difficult task – to solve your problems. Try instead to use the very simple means he gave you: a look, speech, and gesture...'

7 October

You have an extraordinary instrument at your disposal: thought. But why don't you use it? Instead you are content to grumble about all the things you lack. You need beauty, poetry, silence, smiles, kind looks, and kind words? Well, instead of complaining about the fact that people are not giving you these, know that you can create them instantly through thought. You might say, 'But there's nothing; I can't see anything, I can't feel anything.' Of course, if you wait to see them materialized, it will probably take centuries. But they exist in the mental plane. And this is the reality you should hold on to.

Imagine a hypnotist gives you a piece of paper, saying, 'Here is a rose. Smell it.' You will go into raptures over the wonderful fragrance of this rose. How is this possible? You have captured his thought, and his thought, together with the words he has used, has already created the rose in the subtle plane. He has succeeded in projecting your consciousness to the subtle plane and you smell the rose with your psychic sense of smell. So, why not use this method on yourself to extricate yourself from your negative states?

8 October

*M*atter tends towards the spirit; it wants to rise to meet it, in order to become purer and more subtle. And, conversely, the spirit descends towards matter in order to incarnate and manifest through it. In this way, the beloved departs to meet her beloved, who descends from the heavenly regions, and when they meet somewhere in space, they unite in joy!

In the same way, the work of the spiritualist can be characterized by this same process: the meeting of spirit and matter. Whatever they do, whatever their concerns, experiences or plans, they must lead to what I summarize here for you in these words: 'the spiritualization of matter and the incarnation of the spirit'. For when the spirit descends into the depths of a human being, it transforms the raw material of their passions into beauty, purity, light, nobility and love.

9 October

*E*very day, the stock exchange publishes the share prices: some are rising, others are falling, those that are rising today may fall tomorrow, and vice versa. Yes, and on a larger scale, the same phenomena have taken place in the history of the world: at any given time, certain values were held high, and others were not taken into consideration.

In certain eras, for example, physical courage was glorified: heroes were those who knew how to fight each other in tournaments, duels or wars, and who were never afraid of danger. In other times, sacrifice was accorded the highest worth: people admired men and women who could give up everything in order to serve the poor, the sick and the persecuted. In our times, it is the intellect that is most highly valued: the capacity to reason and acquire knowledge in order to act on matter. But this will not last, and already another value is making its appearance: brotherhood. It is this that will motivate human beings to keep expanding their consciousness, so as to acquire the consciousness of universality.

10 October

*T*o justify clumsy words or gestures, many people say, 'I don't know what happened, I lost my head!' And this explanation is sufficient for them. Actually, what we lose in those situations is the connection with the divine world, which is responsible for regulating, coordinating and harmonisation of all elements and activities. This is then followed by disorder and disarray, gestures, glances and words that go in all directions.

If the connection with heaven is no longer present, the cells of your body learn that the head, the boss, is not there anymore. And from then on they no longer feel they must respect the order and harmony you have succeeded in establishing within you, and they act like enemies and threaten you. Where once they were submissive and obedient, now nothing holds them back – you are ill in bed, you make error after error or you suffer, and your cells are delighted to say, 'Aha, aha, very good, this will teach you for having broken the connection with the world of light'. But if you get your head back and re-establish the connection, they set to work together in perfect harmony once again.

11 October

*B*oth within and without, human beings are constantly involved in the battle between the principle of life and the principle of death. These two opposing powers are constantly confronting each other and it is always the weakness of one that makes the strength of the other. When a kingdom is powerful and prospers, all its enemies keep their distance. But as soon as it begins to weaken through the negligence of its governors or the unwillingness of citizens, the enemies take the opportunity to attack and destroy it.

Well the same happens within us, as enemies are always threatening to weaken us by taking away our peace, our inspiration and our courage; they await the slightest moment of inattention on our part. This is why we must be aware of our inner states so as to be able to stand up immediately against these hostile forces. Since we have come to earth to carry out some work, we must not let forces of death become victorious. We must help the powers of life as much as we can, through knowledge, faith, hope and love, so that they may triumph within us.

12 October

*S*top searching for proofs of the existence of God where you will never find them. Look for God within yourself, and you will realize that he is always there, that he never leaves you. If you do not feel him, it is not because he does not exist or is not there, but because you have turned away from him. You have not been attentive to his presence, you have not been sensible, or you have committed certain errors which have deviated you from the path that leads to him, in turn clouding your consciousness. And this now brings about sensations which mislead you about the reality of things.

The Lord is always there, but if you have momentarily allowed your awareness of his presence to be dulled, it will of course seem as if he does not exist. Do your best to get back on to the path of light, and you will once again know that God dwells within you.

13 October

The most serious failing of human beings, the one which creates the greatest obstacle to their evolution, is their unshakeable belief in the infallibility of their reasoning and their points of view. They protect their positions; they cultivate them and defend them.

You might say, 'But the whole world has this failing!' It is true and the most widespread flaw is people's insistence on clinging to their ways of feeling and seeing things, as if there were nothing better or more true than their opinions and beliefs. They do not ask themselves where their convictions come from, or why they hold some and not others, but instead allow themselves to be swept along blindly. And this explains why the earth is becoming a stage for every kind of confrontation, with each person seeking the success of their own point of view inspired by their interests, desires, whims, or simply their moods. Why do human beings have to suffer great catastrophes before they finally recognise they have made errors in judgement and acted out of shameful motives?

14 October

*F*aced with the misfortunes humanity is suffering, people everywhere are complaining that the world is in a terrible state. They talk, they criticise, they protest and become irritated; and while they are preoccupied with their arguments, complaints, and anger, evil continues its course of action. In their opinion, God is responsible, since he does nothing to stop it, despite their prayers.

I have often told you that the so-called devil has one quality, and only one, but it is an extraordinary quality: he is active, energetic, and tireless, whereas people are weak and tire quickly. They think it is enough to be kind and inoffensive; when they have done a few good deeds, they are satisfied with themselves and then must rest. Who knows when they will get back to work. Good does not stimulate them in the same way that evil stimulates criminals. But whose fault is that? It is not God who prevents them from cultivating generosity and selflessness and working for the good of all their fellow human beings.

15 October

Atheists think that they show objectivity, lucidity and reasoning: they think that they at least judge according to what they see, hear, touch, measure and so on, unlike believers who they see as being so obsessed by their faith that they are incapable of being lucid. Well, no, however intelligent a person may be, if they do not accept the existence of God, the reality of the soul and the immortality of the spirit, they will always lack an essential element to complete their observations and judgments. The absence of this element limits them, for they pay too much attention to form, to the surface of life.

An atheist is like someone who, looking at a human being, considers only their anatomy. As long as it is only a question of identifying the limbs and organs, and describing their aspects, anatomy can suffice. But only considering anatomy means taking interest in a body without taking into account the life that animates it. Only the belief in the life of the soul and spirit, and of a divine world where they have their origins, can give humans the true dimension of beings and things and the consciousness of the currents that circulate within them.

16 October

*I*n order to solve certain problems, it is sometimes helpful to forget them for a while and try to think of something else. You might say, 'But if we try to forget about our problems, we will never find the solution!' This is exactly where you are mistaken. It is not because you are obsessed with your difficulties that you will manage to solve them or get rid of them; on the contrary, it is often the best way to encourage them and to let yourself become overwhelmed.

So try to put your problems aside for a moment; find the conditions which will allow you to do great inner work, to rise by means of thought high into the world of light, and there you will find solutions. It is often said that night brings counsel. Yes, because during sleep we forget everything, and a work goes on in the subconscious that then allows us to see more clearly. So, from time to time, are you not able to do the same thing consciously?

17 October

*T*o become true creators, people must call on certain faculties within themselves in order to contact the spiritual world, because it is from the spiritual world that they receive what we call inspiration.

It is important to know what conditions are favourable for inspiration, because inspiration does not visit us by chance. You remark that you have experienced inspiration in rather unlikely situations, places, or postures. Yes, this can happen: you are peeling vegetables, bending down to pick something up or tying your shoelaces, when suddenly a current flows through you, an image comes into your mind, and you know you have had a revelation. On the other hand, you can set up all the material conditions that are ideal for inspiration to visit you, but nothing comes to you at all. Divine inspiration does not necessarily come because you are sitting in the lotus position with your eyes closed, surrounded by clouds of incense. Those are not the conditions I am talking about. The first prerequisite necessary for inspiration is to ensure your thoughts, feelings and actions are pure. When the ground has been prepared, the spirit can visit you no matter what situation or posture you find yourself in.

18 October

*S*o much horror has been perpetrated by people claiming to act out of their love of God. Today, as a result, those who speak of this love increasingly attract only suspicion. Now people think they must look to their fellow human beings, and abandon this remote divinity that has long provided a pretext to persecute them.

But the truth is that if we do not learn to love God first, we will not know how to love other human beings, for our love will be neither intelligent nor enlightened. We must not place so much trust in what comes from the human heart, for although it certainly contains good things, it also contains greed, violence and possessiveness. The human heart is a dark cavern from which all sorts of monsters can emerge, so we must purify and enlighten it, which we can do only if we learn to turn towards the Creator. In order to maintain the right orientation, even when we are thinking of our fellow human beings, we must never forget the Creator.

19 October

*H*uman existence can be compared to a journey through a forest or the ascent of a great mountain. What efforts we must make and what dangers we must confront before we arrive at the goal! And if we undertake this journey or this ascent in darkness, the risk of losing our way, of dangerous encounters, or of falling to the bottom of a precipice is great. In darkness, not only are we truly exposed to danger, but the greatest danger is the fear that we create ourselves, not knowing what to make of the noises and the shadowy forms we see stirring around us. To be afraid is to give power to that which we fear, to prepare the conditions it needs to do harm.

Symbolically, this is the life of human beings when they do not possess true knowledge. Only true knowledge which accompanies them like a light can give them security and peace. Once they have this light, even if they have hardships to endure, since they will see things as they are, they will continue to walk with confidence.

20 October

As long as human beings place such importance on material gain and social position, they will always be in conflict with one another. For there is a limited amount that can be acquired in the physical realm, and it is impossible for the whole world to bathe in opulence. But this does not mean that the whole world cannot be happy, for in fact happiness is not opulence.

It takes very few material goods to provide for our existence and for us to be happy, but only if we understand that we must work to orient our needs toward the psychic world, and beyond to the spiritual world, where the possibilities are infinite. There, each of us can eat and drink all we want without fear of being in conflict with our neighbours or being robbed of our wealth.

21 October

Nothing is more poetic than the beginning of a love affair. A man and a woman meet, they smile at each other, exchange a few words or notice each other from afar and suddenly they feel inspired and become poetical within. But as soon as this love becomes physical, their feelings of wonder start to fade. How many people have noticed this! Yes, they have noticed it, but they do not draw any lessons from it: they make no effort to protect their blossoming love by remaining in the subtle regions for as long as possible.

Through curiosity and greed, men and women seek to go out immediately and explore the terrain, and even what lies beneath! Then, of course, things are no longer the same. They do not appreciate each other in the same way and are no longer in wonder, one for the other, as they know each other too well in situations which were not always the most attractive. Why do they not try to keep a certain distance between them so as to live as long as possible in the world of beauty, poetry, and light?

22 October

When a virtuoso interprets a piece of music, a student sits an exam or a tightrope walker performs their act, if all the energies within them were not concentrated and in harmony, the virtuoso would play false notes, the student would make mistakes and the tightrope walker would break their neck. Because as soon as there is dissipation and dissonance within, all the inner forces let go and scatter, and the person is no longer supported.

You have often experienced this type of thing, but have you ever stopped to consider how this affects the whole of life? If you give in to haste, disorder and agitation, the forces and entities of harmony within you are repressed and paralyzed. Therefore, several times a day, stop for a few minutes and try to introduce harmony within you. All the forces, all the good entities that have until then not had a chance to manifest, will then be mobilized and available to help you continue your work.

23 October

A mantra, a sacred formula, is like a mould that must be filled with intense life, that is to say, with love and faith. And because sound acts on matter, it is important to say this mantra out loud. It is true that saying something out loud can be seen as just air in motion, but for invisible forces to act, words are necessary. When spoken aloud, a formula releases currents that rise up through the heavenly hierarchies to the throne of God. We must pronounce it at least three times, so that it can have an effect on the three worlds: physical, psychic and spiritual.

Tireless repetition of the same formula penetrates the depths of the subconscious where the roots of our being are found and it is here, in the roots, that we have great possibilities for transformation.

24 October

When people meet artists – painters, poets, musicians – whose works they admire, they are often surprised to discover that the person and their behaviour are completely devoid of the beauty found in their creations: they emanate neither light, nor poetry, nor harmony. Why? Because for the most part, artists are content to create works outside themselves using materials exterior to themselves. It is on these outer materials that they concentrate their efforts. Well, this is insufficient. Art must not merely be confined to somewhere within the creation, but it must also exist in daily life. The true artist is one who can see themselves as material for their creation.

All the methods of the spiritual life are at our disposal, to help and inspire us in this work. Yes, it is within ourselves first and foremost that we must create poetry and music, harmonious forms and movements and shimmering colours, so that all those around us, in the visible and invisible worlds alike, can benefit from them.

25 October

*B*ecause there are so many machines, instruments and products that do everything for us and make our lives effortless, human beings are sinking deeper and deeper into laziness, both physical and mental. How much activity, how many exercises of endurance or willpower have they given up since the invention of cars, elevators, washing machines, calculators, computers – and medicines!

Of course, I approve of all this progress, because I too benefit from all the advantages that come with it. The thing is that if human beings are not careful, they will become accustomed to not making any effort and will always wait for some new machine or product to be invented to make things even easier for them... until their will becomes totally paralyzed. If human beings are to develop correctly, they must make an effort every day; they must not stop doing some physical activity, and especially should continue their mental and psychic activities. No matter what area of our life, we must never give in to finding the easy way out.

26 October

*T*o improve oneself is a difficult undertaking, and many abandon the work when they see what slow progress they are making, whereas others, disappointed with themselves, are in despair. Well, the first are weak and lazy, and the others are proud. There is no point in losing hope when you see that you are far from living up to the magnificent image that you dreamed of for yourself. You must be humble and say, 'Alright, you are not successful this time, and maybe you will not succeed next time, but that is no reason to stop trying.'

You must never lose the desire to progress. It is not the end of the world if you fall down, but each time you must make the effort to get up again. In all circumstances of life, what is most important is to hold onto the will and desire to continue improving oneself. There are always improvements to be made. And the idea of perfection is an inseparable part of human existence.

27 October

*T*o desire privileges and powers that others do not have is an innate tendency of human nature. And there are many ways people can dominate others: if they cannot succeed on the physical plane, they attempt it on the psychic plane. Lacking other means of control, people motivated by ambition, greed and fanaticism have used religion to dominate their fellow humans psychologically. So we cannot help but observe that religion has too often become an institution with little concern for spirituality, and that it is no longer able to offer salvation to the faithful.

Fortunately, the Creator has marked each human being with his seal. This mark is inscribed deeply within them, and allows them, whenever they truly desire, to discover in their heart and soul that which religion does not take the trouble to reveal. If they look for this seal within themselves, they will find salvation.

28 October

Jesus said, *'Just as I have loved you, you also should love one another.'* What was the nature of Jesus' love? What did he see in a human being? The response is found in the Sermon on the Mount when he addressed his disciples and the crowd that had followed him, and said, *'Be perfect as your heavenly Father is perfect.'* What this means is that in his disciples and in all those who came to him, Jesus saw the image of the heavenly Father, of the Divinity, and it was to this Divinity within them that he addressed himself as he showed them the path to perfection.

While the scribes and Pharisees only saw the pitiful appearance of all the paralytics, the lepers, the possessed, prostitutes, adulterers, thieves, and so on, Jesus recognised in all beings a soul and a spirit that simply asked for the conditions to allow the manifestation of their beauty and light. It was these souls and these spirits that he loved, and it was to them that he spoke. And he asks us to do likewise.

29 October

Suppose you have an icon or a holy picture at home: morning and evening you light a candle in front of it, you pray and ask it to protect you. But it is not the icon itself that will protect you. What will protect you is the inner state induced within you by your prayer, the effects of which remain imprinted in you and guide you in the way of light, love, and peace.

You are therefore the only one who can really do something for yourself, through the connection you make with heaven. Statues or holy pictures are only a starting point, a support.

30 October

Ageing is often seen as a trial. Yes it is not pleasant to lose the physical and intellectual capacities you once possessed. But old age can also be the best stage of one's life. For those who have nourished a high ideal during their youth and adulthood, many things improve during old age: understanding and lucidity, for example. How can this be explained? It can be said that the subtle bodies did not follow the same processes as the physical body. The legs, the eyes and the ears of the elderly begin to betray them, as does their brain in some ways, but the life of their soul and spirit becomes increasingly rich and abundant. It is as if they have finally tasted the fruits of their efforts.

So, prepare yourselves, think about enriching yourself within while you are still young, so that later you may taste this abundance of fruits.

31 October

A disciple who goes to listen to their master or who immerses themself for a few hours in studying their master's thoughts, feels themself transported into a world of light, purity and love. But then, unavoidably, they return to everyday life where they are obliged to meet all types of people and face all manner of situations. After a while, they notice they no longer have the same faith or the same enthusiasm; they feel that they have once again become dull and heavy, and that their ardour and love have diminished. What has happened? Like a hot liquid that is then exposed to the cold, their temperature has changed. This phenomenon is completely natural. The teaching a disciple receives from a master resembles the contents of a container. Symbolically, the contents are warmer than the prevailing atmosphere, and when they come in contact with it, their temperature gradually drops.

But what is lost can always be replaced. This is the purpose of prayer, meditation and all spiritual practices: to seek at the source those luminous and warmth-giving elements that you have lost.

1 November

Most people readily admit that in order to succeed in the material world, you must be committed and work without cutting corners. But in the spiritual realm they imagine they can obtain results easily and quickly. What a mistake! In the spiritual realm, more so than in the material world, you must first set to work and never relax your effort. Secondly, you must not be in a hurry, because it is a long-term undertaking and time is not a factor. Finally, you must have faith: be convinced that this spiritual work will one day bear fruit, because nature is faithful and true, and the laws which govern it can never be faulted.

Work, time and faith. You do not realise the wealth contained in these three words. We can, of course, present them in a different order: faith, work, and time, and so on. What is essential is to understand that these three elements are connected, and to know how they are connected.

2 November

*I*f the Church has instituted what is referred to as 'the last sacraments' or 'the extreme unction' it is because the moment at which an individual leaves the earth for the other world is of vital importance. The aim is to prepare the soul for the long journey it is about to undertake. The priest or pastor tries to bring the person back to the fundamental issues: they explain it is time to look back at their life, to take stock of their errors, to repent, and to find within them the bond that unites them with the Creator. Some will think it is a little late. Yes, no doubt it is a little late, but it is not too late. Because those who leave their physical body without having prepared themselves for it, without having the faintest notion of life after death, of divine Justice, subsequently suffer greatly because they roam the dark regions of the beyond without understanding what is happening to them.

It is very bad to keep human beings in the mistaken conviction that there is nothing after death. Under the pretext of freeing them from absurd beliefs, on the contrary, they are being prepared for hardships in the other world that are far worse than those they have had to suffer on earth.

3 November

*B*ecause God is so great, he neither concerns himself with the mistakes and malice of human beings, nor does he vary according to their behaviour. Therefore, if you feel worried or rejected because you have behaved badly, do not claim that God has withdrawn or that he has rejected you. Instead, make an effort and rectify your mistakes and you will once again feel close to him.

Above all, do not wait for God to forgive you: he has not condemned you, so he has nothing to forgive you for. No purpose is served by beating your breast and saying, 'I am a sinner. I am a sinner.' Since you had the power to create the clouds that deprive you of God's light, you also have the power to disperse them. Everything depends on you, on your attitude. What good do all the advancements in psychology serve if human beings are not able to analyse these vitally important states they experience, to understand them and correct them?

4 November

What makes a car run? The release of energy generated when the gaseous mixture in the engine explodes when ignited by a spark. The car then starts and will run for as long as there is fuel in the tank.

The same is true with breathing. If we are to extract the maximum energy from the air that passes through our nostrils, we must compress it by holding it in our lungs. While this compression takes place, our body is at work, activating processes equivalent to ignition and combustion in a car. And, as the air cannot escape, nature opens tiny passages in our body through which it can circulate. Thanks to this retention, energy contained in the air passes through all of these little channels made especially for it by nature, who says to it, 'This way… that way…' for along its route nature has placed certain subtle centres – the chakras – which can be activated only through contact with this energy.

5 November

*T*he higher world and the lower world are not separate; in both the universe and in human beings, there are connections between these two worlds. That is why, when humans have a very elevated, very spiritual wish, it can provoke their lower nature which then immediately raises opposing forces. The magnificent things you desire on high awaken contradictory forces and desires in the roots of your being! These tricks of the lower nature triumph with much greater difficulty in the disciple who understands and is enlightened, because they know they must take precautions. While they build their inner temple, they pray to have around them, beings that watch over and protect them.

In early freemasonry, whose philosophy was based on a true science, the mason was represented working with a trowel in one hand, and in the other a sword with which to defend themself. So, while the mason is busy building, they are also vigilant and make sure that in the cover of darkness certain enemies do not try to worm their way into their fortress. And if they do try to enter, the mason wards them off with their sword.

6 November

What can you add to a receptacle that is already full? Nothing. In order to pour something else into it, it must first be emptied. The same applies to human beings: if they do not empty themselves of their weaknesses and bad habits, how can divine virtues and qualities come and establish themselves within them? This is the meaning of renunciation: to renounce is to empty oneself and to get rid of certain elements which are harmful to oneself and to others, so that something that is purer and is filled with more light can be introduced to take their place.

Those who have understood the meaning of renunciation strive to create this necessary void, so that divine qualities come and live within them. They must stop thinking that they will be unhappy if they give up certain pleasures. On the contrary, these insignificant pleasures will be replaced by others that are far greater, and of better quality.

7 November

A man is sitting quietly somewhere, his face expresses nothing in particular. But suddenly an impulse comes from deep down inside: a thought, a feeling of fear, love, anger... and then everything changes, his features, the expression of his face, the color of his skin. How can the physical body suddenly change under the impulse of something so impalpable and subtle as a thought or a feeling? Just one emotion, and we blush, or go pale, or are petrified! Sometimes people die because of an emotion. How can an emotion have such power over the physical body?

Everyone is aware of these phenomena, so why have they never drawn the conclusion that it is the psychic life that commands the physical life? The physical body always depends on a psychic or spiritual element above it, which creates or destroys, expands or contracts, which tints, which shapes... Of course it is always possible to influence the body by physical means; they can momentarily improve your health or appearance. But health and beauty depend far more on your thoughts, feelings and on everything making up your inner life.

8 November

When you feel anxious or distressed, react and keep your thoughts from taking a dangerous downhill direction, catch them and force them to return to this place of light and peace in you that is sheltered from adversity. If you are not vigilant, you have no idea to where an instant of anger, fear, resentment, or discouragement may lead you.

Watch a trapeze artiste or the tightrope walker: how they move freely in the air. But in order to do so, how they have worked! They have this freedom of movement because they have learned not to allow themself to become distracted by extraneous elements which would cost them their concentration and send them hurtling to the ground. In order to remain in the heights, you too must protect your consciousness from disturbances. At the slightest warning, ensure that your thoughts do not stray from the regions of light and inner calm.

9 November

When a woman is pregnant, dark entities from the invisible world seek to enter through an open door in her and settle in her child. A mother, through her behaviour, is the one who opens and closes the doors. When a pregnant woman feels thoughts, desires or chaotic feelings pass through her that she has never had before, she must be aware this is proof that dark entities are lingering close by. If she does not resist them or protect herself, these entities will enter the child who will then be visited by these entities throughout their life and be prey to them.

If we are to prepare the best possible future for the young generations to come, it is important to know the realities of the psychic world. A mother therefore needs to be vigilant and to find the 'keys', that is to say the light-filled thoughts and feelings, that will close the door to the dark entities, and she will be able to protect her child. As for those close to a mother-to-be – her husband, parents, friends, neighbours, work colleagues – they also need to know this and try to create an atmosphere of peace and harmony around her.

10 November

*M*ost people devote their days to the satisfaction of their desires and the realization of their ambitions. Do they ever question the nature of all these calculations, designs and projects? Do they ever think to turn to heavenly beings and ask, 'O luminous spirits, are we in harmony with your plans? What is your opinion? What do you have in mind for us? Where and how must we work to accomplish your will?' Very few ask themselves these questions.

Nothing, however, is more important for a human being than to ask the beings of light in the invisible world to enable them one day to carry out the projects of heaven. Because at that very moment, their whole life changes: they are no longer guided by their whims, their weaknesses, and their blindness. In their efforts to know divine will, they put themself on a different track; they take a direction which corresponds to God's plans, and that is the true life!

11 November

*F*aced with some failures, you might feel discouraged to the point that you tell yourself, 'I am incompetent, weak and stupid.' Very well, you may well be all that, but it is dangerous for you to dwell on it. When you experience states of this kind, show that you still have a little intelligence and make efforts to think, 'All right, I may not amount to much, but there is a world of rich, beautiful, and wise beings, and I am going to unite with them by means of thought in order to benefit from their qualities and virtues.' I assure you that this will help you.

Also, try to recall all the wonderful moments of peace, light, and inspiration that you have already experienced, for you have experienced at least some. And since you have experienced them, they cannot be wiped out. Cling to those moments, and little by little, courage and faith will return to you.

12 November

*E*ach of you must understand that you are a spiritual entity who lives in relationship with the universe, and that you can obtain everything you need from the inexhaustible worlds of the soul and spirit. This will give your life meaning, and you will no longer feel the need to run after ephemeral gains.

So beware: even if nowadays social and material success appear ever more convincingly to be the only ways to guarantee your security, you must not give them priority. Sooner or later you will be forced to admit that this security was an illusion and that in searching for it at all costs, you have wasted a lot of time and energy. If your worth and competency have been recognised and you are offered an important position in any field whatsoever, accept it if you wish. But be vigilant, and never abandon what is essential: the wealth you can gain in the world of the soul and the spirit.

13 November

*H*ow many believers ask why heaven does not intervene to restore order in world affairs! Well, this shows they are not good psychologists. Without the agreement and willingness of human beings themselves, what is the use of the interventions of heaven? People would neither understand nor appreciate this new order established by heaven and would quickly destroy it. The desire for change must come from human beings.

Yes, if they truly wish to remedy the state of things and right the misfortune in the world, because of what they have suffered and the lessons they have learned, heaven will release other forces, other currents, other energies, and then true changes will take place. But the impulse must come from human beings; they must decide together to work in order to obtain the intervention of cosmic forces. If they do not provide the right conditions for them to intervene, nothing will happen and the sublime intelligences will never decide to get mixed up in human affairs.

14 November

How to get along with others is the most important problem that human beings have to solve every day. Work on yourself, therefore, in order to develop the psychic and moral qualities which will allow you to better understand and accept others. For this is essential; to learn to live with all the others, and not only with your family, your friends, your neighbours, your colleagues, those close to you and so on. You must also be able to relate to all sorts of people who differ from you in age, education, social class, nationality and race,* in order to become accustomed very early on to all human situations.

You cannot know ahead of time the encounters life is preparing for you. So unless you are ready and one day are required to face these situations, you will appear closed, unsympathetic, intolerant and sometimes, unintentionally, even mean. Yes, the measure of a person's evolution is their capacity to meet others and relate harmoniously with them.

* See note page 175.

15 November

You should not ask that a spiritual master be all-knowing and all-powerful. You have the right to ask only one thing of them: that they serve as a link to heaven for you, that they guide you on the path of light, that they show you the way to God.

Moreover, a true spiritual master will not keep you for themself; they will take you further, higher. And if you insist upon staying close to them, they will tell you, 'No, do not count so much on me. I cannot give you everything. Only God can fulfil you. I can only help you to find the path. If you like, I am like a telephone that enables you to communicate with the divine world, with the heavenly hierarchies, and that is all.' That is what a true master will say. If they are not a true master, of course, they will make all kinds of promises that will never come true, so it is up to you to be discerning.

16 November

You still do not make use of the many opportunities given to you to unite with the divine world in order to calm yourself and recover your inner balance. And yet, you know very well that the agitation of daily life eventually weakens your nervous system. Human beings are not made to live in this constant tension that drains them of all their energies. It is not normal to run from morning to evening or to be harassed from all sides, and you eventually become worn out, both physically and psychically.

Several times a day, therefore, stop for a few moments. Concentrate and try to create an atmosphere of harmony and love within you and around you. By repeating this exercise often, you will succeed in touching your higher self which will project beneficial rays into all your cells. It is thus that you will restore balance and be able to deal with all your daily tasks again.

17 November

There is nothing to be greatly admired in the many brilliant, wealthy and powerful people who place no importance on the life of the soul and spirit. Because they do not seek spiritual nourishment, which alone could fulfil them, they are like starving beasts; and their ambition, greed and voracity finally lead them down paths that are dangerous both for themselves and for those around them.

Unfortunately, many so-called spiritualists do not behave any better: they try to satisfy their ambitions and gain the same success as the materialists by the means given to them by Initiatic Science. In doing so they betray the most sacred principles and are thus even more guilty than the materialists. It is clear that they are satisfied and proud of succeeding by these means, but heaven, which does not like to be used for egotistical and self-interested ends, will one day ask them to account for their deeds, and they will be severely punished.

18 November

When you invite someone to stay with you for a few days, you prepare a room for them. You do not just say, 'Come, come', without knowing where you are going to put them. All the more so if your guest is someone important. Before extending your invitation, you think about how you are going to welcome them.

Imagine, for instance, that you are expecting a prince or princess to come and stay: are you going to let them go through a dirty, untidy house? Well, believers please forgive me, if I say they treat God in ways they would not dare to treat even their neighbours. They pray to him, 'Come, Lord'. But, do they prepare a place for the Creator within themselves, a sacred place? No, they invite him to a place that is a total shambles, to a dung heap. Later they are astonished when it is not God who comes to visit them, but some devils who themselves feel quite at home amongst impurities.

19 November

When you feel hatred for someone, what is this force that teaches you to pulverise them with a look or even to strike them? And if you love someone tenderly, what is this force that moves you to smile at them, to speak sweetly to them, to hold them tight in your arms and to bring them gifts?

Whether it is love or hate, it is always the same force: sometimes it manifests in the Venusian form and acts with delicacy, expressiveness, poetry, and gentleness, and sometimes it becomes Martian and can shatter everything in its path. Just observe how love which manifests in too low a form can turn into violence. The need to satisfy their desires makes men and women egotistical and cruel, and they do not care about the other person, and are even ready to kill them if they resist. On the contrary, those who wish to manifest the higher degrees of love act with generosity and selflessness, and with consideration for the fulfilment and happiness of the person they love. And yet, in its origins, the force is the same.

20 November

'Everyone then who hears these words of mine and acts on them will be like a wise man who built his house on a rock', said Jesus. *'And everyone who hears these words of mine and does not act on them will be like a foolish man who built his house on sand.'* What is this house? It is an image of human beings themselves: if they found their existence on sand, that is to say on unstable ground which will quake with their chaotic thoughts and feelings, it will endlessly sway and eventually collapse.

If our life is to stand firm, we must build it on this rock which represents our higher mental body, the causal plane*. As its name – causal – indicates, it is from this plane that the currents flow which influence the mental, astral and physical realms. This explains why the work we can accomplish by rising to the causal plane has repercussions on our thoughts, our feelings, our daily behaviour, and even on our health, as if orders were given from on high to bring order and harmony to our entire being.

* See note and diagram, p. 400 and 401.

21 November

Whatever your circumstances, always remember to analyze yourself so that you know what you are doing, and especially how you are doing it.

For example, every day you are obliged to do certain tasks that are more or less interesting or pleasant. But, pleasant and interesting or not, they have to be done. So, observe carefully how you set about doing a job you do not like very much: you sigh, you grumble, and you go at it without conviction or love, thinking perhaps it was a job for others. You do not realize that your attitude makes the work even more difficult. And then, not only do the efforts you are required to make bring you nothing inwardly, but they destroy you. Whereas if you learn to consider things in another way, if you decide you are going to use this boring work as a chance to become stronger or more intelligent, you will change your state of consciousness and the task will seem less painful.

22 November

*B*efore leaping into a task of some importance, try to study the situation carefully. Weigh the pros and cons and even ask for advice, until everything is very clear to you. The blind faith of those who rush into things can only lead to failure. When people do not want to see the reality around them and refuse to take into account all aspects of a situation, they can only fail. Determination is one thing and obstinacy is another. So many undertakings have failed despite the absolute confidence the people had! They lacked experience, they had not properly studied the various aspects of the situation. They imagined that to be motivated with the best intentions and to be completely confident and willing were enough to guarantee success, and that heaven would take care of the rest. No, that is not enough.

But once you have thought it through and you see things clearly, you must not hesitate for one moment: you must put aside the slightest doubt so that you are able not only to act appropriately but to persevere whatever the difficulties.

23 November

*I*n esoteric science, the white and black lodge are the two lodges that operate in the universe. The powers we generally call 'good' and 'evil' are those of the light and the dark. But the two lodges are dominated by a third lodge, of which even the initiates know very little, for it is a reality that is beyond human understanding. This third lodge is the exclusive domain of God, who is above both good and evil, and who uses them both.

Human beings must not seek to combat the black lodge as they are not armed for this fight. The only thing we can do is to remain connected to the white lodge, to the powers of good and follow their instructions: they will confer on us the elements that will neutralise the secret poisons of the black lodge. And in this way, we will be able to make good triumph while maintaining our strength and peace.

24 November

*H*uman beings do not seem to be aware that their attitude toward the divine world determines their destiny. Increasingly, instead of bowing before the grandeur of God and glorifying him, they are adopting careless and disrespectful behaviours which thwart his plans and introduce chaos in his creation.

The worst enemy of human beings is pride, this self-important and arrogant attitude which will eventually lead to their ruin. If they want to save themselves, they must learn to regard creation as sacred, to vibrate like the Aeolian harp with each breath of wind, with each current from heaven, to commune with the universe, with the universal Soul and with the cosmic Spirit. During this exchange, energies from the higher world work on them: elements of the greatest purity flow into their soul, while the dark elements leave and are absorbed in immensity.

25 November

*B*ecause it has a synthetic view of reality, intuition is true intelligence. It does not need to do research or calculations, its understanding is instantaneous; it penetrates everything with a single glance – the objective and subjective worlds, the exterior and interior – and transmits its findings directly to you.

Intuition is both a feeling and an understanding; you feel things at the same time as you understand them. It is a higher intelligence because it comprehends, in a single moment, the whole of life. And when everyone else is still hesitating and doubting, those who possess this intelligence understand immediately and their vision is infallible. And when reality appears to them in this way – with both aspects, objective and subjective, exterior and interior – they are amazed to discover that everything is in fact very simple.

26 November

*I*n your prayers and meditations, begin by trying to reach the saints, the prophets, the initiates and the great masters, that is, those beings whose mission it is to take care of human beings. Then, you can rise further and invoke the angels because, in the celestial hierarchies, angels are the closest to human beings, and they can hear them and help them. You can also try to invoke the Archangels, but don't seek to go any higher: the Principalities, the Powers, the Dominions, the Thrones, the Cherubim and the Seraphim, they will not hear you.

There are countless worlds in infinite space inhabited by thousands of beings, and these angelic hierarchies, which have very important work to carry out far away in space, have very little to do with human beings. Those who look after humans are for the most part beings who have lived on earth and have left it, but who remember it: they are still connected to it and have made promises which they intend to keep. You must know that the higher hierarchies exist. You can try to connect to them by pronouncing their names, but know that you will only be heard by the beings but who are closest to human beings.

27 November

*Y*ou may become a victim of grave injustices on the part of human beings. If you are really innocent, do everything you can within to resist. Never give anyone the opportunity to harm you or destroy you. Why do you care about what these people think if they are so blind? Just listen to the judgement of the inner tribunal of your conscience, the Divinity that lives within you.

Be concerned above all with being clear about yourself, and always behave with honesty and disinterestedness. Then, tell yourself that who you are; your dignity and your honour, do not depend on what others think of you. Your divine nature supports you, and this should be enough for you to continue walking with your head held high.

28 November

You may, as you are walking down the street, without knowing it, pass through a place where a dishonest deed or even a crime is being committed. If, at that particular moment, you happen to find yourself in a negative inner state or with negative thoughts, you resonate with the vibrations produced by such deeds and fall under their influence. You may then be pushed into doing wrong yourself, without actually realizing it is because of the fluidic emanations you received as you walked by.

This is why it is so important for you to watch the quality of your inner states, because it is the only effective way to protect yourself from dark influences. Do not rely on amulets, talismans or any other kind of trinket offered to you by charlatans. It is down to you; you have to work on your thoughts and feelings so that you may attract only fragrances of purity and light. These are the true amulets that will protect you.

29 November

*I*n anticipation of the approaching winter we all know we must prepare ourselves to face the cold: we think about preparing in terms of the heating, the insulation of our houses, warmer clothes, and so on. Unfortunately, people have far less foresight when it comes to facing the winters within them, and when a dark period befalls them, they are defenceless and can only complain that life has no meaning.

It is true that the seasons of the inner life do not return with the same regularity as those of nature, and that they are therefore not predictable. But winter inevitably returns from time to time, and if you learn to observe yourself, each time you will discover certain warning signals within you. So, as soon as you feel this time of cold and darkness approaching, be careful. Prepare the spiritual elements that will continue to sustain the fire and the light within you. Jesus said, *'Walk while you have the light, so that the darkness does not surprise you.'* This means: make the most of good conditions to arm yourself against the day when you need to face difficulties.

30 November

*S*ilence is the essential condition that allows us to hear the true word, true revelations. In silence, little by little you feel the messages from the spiritual world reach you, a voice seeks to warn you, to give you advice, to guide you, to protect you...

You might say that you don't hear this voice. It is because you are making too much noise, not only on the physical level, but also on the astral and mental levels*: there are so many chaotic feelings and thoughts that constantly clash within you. This voice that speaks to you is called 'the voice of silence', and it even appears as the title of certain books of oriental wisdom. When the yogi manages to calm everything within themself and to stop the flow of their thoughts – because in its movement, thought also creates noise – they then hear this voice of silence which is the very voice of God.

* See note and diagram, p. 400 and 401.

1 December

We hear people everywhere complain that the world is in a bad way. And there they go complaining, all they do is complain and they expect others to set to work and improve conditions. Why do they not begin it themselves? No, they wait, and others do the same and wait too... and this can go on forever.

You might say that faced with the immensity of the tasks to be done, you feel discouraged. Well, on the contrary, you must remain courageous, because it is in doing so that you show yourself to be praiseworthy. In pleasant circumstances it is too easy to believe in good and to set to work: everything is simple and agreeable. It is in difficult times that it is important to commit oneself and to persevere, without allowing oneself to be influenced by the conditions. You must learn to count on the powers of the spirit. This is the sign of the true spiritualist: despite bad conditions, despite the storms, spiritualists always try to awaken the powers of the will, of good, and of the light.

2 December

*E*very manifestation of physical, psychic and spiritual life gives beings specific wave-lengths and vibrations that connect them automatically to entities and currents in space who have the same wave-lengths and currents. This explains the connections we have with forces of nature. We resonate with certain regions and entities with the same wave-lengths through our thoughts, feelings and actions. And through the force of attraction, sooner or later, we are able to come to meet them.

Initiatic Science gives every human being the means with which to create the future they wish. And it is the quality of their thoughts, feelings and desires that draws them towards the darkness and chaos, or towards the pure, light-filled regions of the divine world.

3 December

Spiritual work and the work on oneself is a long and exacting endeavour. When faced with the length of the path to be followed and the obstacles along the way, doubt can creep in and you no longer believe you have the qualities necessary to achieve any results whatsoever. You then feel a kind of division or split within you, and this is very harmful to your psychic life: this terrible self-doubt may gradually paralyze you.

But whatever your reasons for self-doubt, there is only one thing that will prevent this poison from destroying you: the awareness that within you lives a being who is all-powerful, all-knowing and all-loving: the Lord, the Creator of all worlds. And in connecting yourself to him, by relying on him, you can continue to build your inner self.

4 December

*P*roud people imagine they are dependent on nothing and no one, exactly like a light bulb which claims to be the source of light, forgetting that the power station supplies the current. Those who are humble, on the contrary, know that they are not an isolated being, that they are not independent, and that if they do not remain linked to heaven, they will have neither force, light nor wisdom. They sense that they are a link in an infinite chain, the conductor of a cosmic energy which comes from afar and flows through them to all other human beings.

What consequences to these attitudes hold? Proud people forget the source of the currents which manifest through them; they believe they are dependent only upon themself, and sooner or later become a barren land. Humble people are like a valley irrigated by the water that descends from the peaks to fertilise the plains; they receive forces that pour forth constantly from the mountains and thus know abundance. We have not yet understood the wealth of humility.

5 December

We only achieve that which we have already envisioned and prepared in our minds. This is a matter worthy of deep reflection. The way in which we consider people and things is what counts and what is effective, and we can verify this in every domain of life.

For example, if you see the person you share your life with as someone who makes it possible for you to satisfy your material needs, to indulge your vanity, and to unleash your sensuality and desires for pleasure, you are linking yourself to the lower forces of the astral plane*, and you should not be surprised if, one day, you see all your dreams of happiness collapse. On the other hand, if you make the habit of considering this person as a manifestation of divinity, then through you will connect heavenly powers. You will receive great blessings and will be filled with joy.

* See note and diagram, p. 400 and 401.

6 December

*R*oads and paths on land are generally quite congested with traffic, seas and oceans are less so, and flight paths even less; and we can fly through the air at high speeds without coming across any obstacles.

What meaning does this have for us? Those who remain attached to the earth, that is to say who only seek to respond to the calls of their stomach, belly and genitals, come meet many obstacles in their path because they come up against the material considerations of those close to them. If they tell themselves, 'Since that's the way it is, I'll go out onto the water', which corresponds to the astral plane: feelings, emotions, they will move forward more freely, but there they will also come into conflict with other people's desires and passions. 'So then, I'll go up into the air', the mental plane, the domain of thought. It's even better, space opens up more widely before them, but there they will be confronted with people with different philosophical, scientific, religious or political ideas. If they would like to avoid any future obstacles, they need aim to rise above the realm of air, to the subtle, crystal-clear, luminous regions of ether, that is to say to their higher self.

7 December

Life and death are so closely connected that there is always something in life that must die in order for something else to live. Like it or not, it is impossible to escape this dilemma.

We can already observe this in the realm of health. How many sick people who have been advised by their doctors to stop smoking or drinking alcohol to stay alive feel that if they follow this advice, they would feel as if they were dying! Yes, because there are two conflicting ideas of life here: that of the instinctive life and that of the life of reason. If we live one thing, we must renounce another. Those who, on the pretext of living more intensely or more pleasantly, fail to respect the laws of the physical life, become ill and die. You must decide which form of life you prefer, because you cannot live one thing and its opposite at the same time. And this is even more true for the spiritual life.

8 December

*E*ven if human beings object to evil and desire good, they are far more convinced of the power of evil than of good. Experience has shown them, they say, that those who want to destroy others and create disorder succeed more readily and more quickly than those who want to be helpful and redress a situation. If this is the case, why should they make such an effort? They do nothing, or are even influenced to behave badly themselves.

But there is one question that they have not asked themselves: this success that evil has achieved, how long will it last? Yes, in order to draw truly valid conclusions, we must introduce the factor of time: how long will these forces of evil continue to triumph? Because the moment evil is set in motion, the forces of good do not remain inactive: they too rise up to re-establish order and justice.

9 December

'*When you pray, go into your room, close the door, and pray to your Father who is there in the secret place.*' How should we understand this secret room of which Jesus speaks?

When someone succeeds in creating silence and peace within themselves, when they need to express their love for God and to commune with him, they are already in their secret room. You may wonder where this room is: is it perhaps in the heart, in the mind, or in the soul? In fact, it is a level of consciousness which you strive to attain. For example, you are meditating upon a difficult spiritual problem, you go deep within to find an answer and after a while, there is light within you, and you understand. What has happened? Where has this understanding come from? Your spirit had this answer all the time, but your consciousness was not yet ready to rise to it. So this is the meaning of Jesus' words: when someone prays or meditates, they lock themself in their secret room, and there they receive revelations.

10 December

*A*lone, and left to themselves, human beings cannot evolve: they need stimulation from the outside world, from nature, from events, and of course from other human beings. They need to see, to hear, to have encounters, and even to receive shocks and to suffer. If they are not roused, shaken up, they will do nothing.

And what is true on the physical and psychic planes is also true in a more subtle way in the spiritual realm. That is why great masters are so necessary: thanks to their pure lives, to their emanations, to their feelings and thoughts of love and wisdom, these beings succeed in stirring something within us. And if they do not always manage to do so, it is not because they are incapable or weak, but because we have allowed ourselves to become buried under too many layers of dull and heavy matter. In order to allow their force and light to penetrate through us, we have inner work to undertake upon ourselves.

11 December

In all religions, the supreme God is seen as the unique source of life. It is he who gives life, and he who withdraws it. He is the master of life, because he is life. But, what do we know about life? We can do no more than enumerate its many manifestations and say that in it, all things are possible, that it contains all gifts. But as for life itself, it is still a mystery.

As for God, so for life: all our attempts to grasp its secrets are destined to fail. While playing sorcerers' apprentices, biologists in their laboratories may soon have some success in their tinkering, this may delude them for a moment into thinking that they have become masters of life. But they will soon be obliged to acknowledge their failure, for life belongs to God alone. God gives life, but he does not reveal the secret of his creation, it is his secret alone.

12 December

Sometimes, while in the mountains, we see on the edge of a precipice a tree whose trunk and branches are oddly twisted. This tree has had to withstand high winds, bad weather, even lightning, but it resisted and its struggle against the elements is reflected in its trunk and branches. In the same way, in life we meet people whose faces are tortured and asymmetrical, but what gifts, what talents! This proves that they too have had to endure very difficult conditions. And to overcome them, they have often developed their mind and will to the detriment of certain qualities of the heart, and these efforts, these tensions, are visible on their faces.

Beauty in human beings speaks more of the qualities of their heart than of their intellectual faculties or their will. Beauty, true beauty, has a much greater affinity with kindness than with intelligence. This is why very beautiful people are often predestined to be victims. And this is why it is important that they are surrounded by people who can help them to defend themselves against the desires their beauty arouses in others.

13 December

*I*n order to console Christians, the Church tells them, *'You are poor, weak and sick, but have hope and faith, for God's love is infinite, and one day you will be on his right side in Paradise.'* So God's circle must be made up of poor, pitiful wretches dressed in rags! Well no, unfortunately for them... but fortunately for the Lord, he is surrounded only with splendour, with the most luminous, the most powerful and the purest beings. Therefore Christians should not count so much on experiencing in heaven all the bliss they have not known on earth. They should work instead to activate the spiritual powers within them, which will enable them to immediately obtain light, love and joy that they aspire to.

When you sow a seed, the four elements, all the powers of heaven and earth are present to sustain your work, and you will soon have flowers and fruits. But if you have sown nothing, nothing will grow, even if you have hope and faith.

14 December

*I*n the Zodiac, Sagittarius, an archer on horseback, symbolizes the human being in whom reason has triumphed over the dark forces of instinct. This idea is also expressed by the mythological figure of the Centaur, which has the torso of a man mounted on the body of a horse.

The Sagittarius and the Centaur are symbols of human beings who are made up of two natures: inferior and superior, and they must learn how to control them. They cannot rid themselves of their inferior nature but must learn to master it and put it to work. What is more, illustrations of the Centaur or Sagittarius show the body of the horse in motion and galloping. But this motion is not without purpose or direction; it serves a well-considered action, the arrow flies, but not in any direction, it must reach its target. You are aware of the mastery it takes to draw a bow and aim accurately. Sagittarius thus represents one who places the movements of their inferior nature – represented by the galloping horse – at the service of an ideal: symbolized by the arrow which goes precisely to its mark.

15 December

*A*re there many adults who are truly concerned about helping young people become clear-sighted, balanced and strong? No, a great many of them are on the lookout for that which can seduce children and adolescents whose instincts and desires are awakening, and they hasten to satisfy these desires. It begins with toys and then continues with all sorts of objects or activities which are altogether useless or even harmful. Young people would themselves have no idea of such things unless they saw them displayed everywhere in shop windows and promoted by advertising.

So many people are guilty of leading young people astray. First of all, they awaken material needs in the young which cannot be satisfied, which leads to frustration, and the desire to obtain dishonestly what cannot be obtained honestly. Then, by trying to convince them that they absolutely need these objects and activities in order to feel well and happy, they turn them away from the true search for happiness and the meaning of life. These people should not be surprised if one day they have to suffer from the criminal behaviour which they have helped to create and nurture.

16 December

We naturally tend to identify God with good. But in reality no, good is not actually God himself; good is a manifestation of God, but it is not God. God is above good and evil, and we cannot really know who he is. But since good represents for us the highest manifestation of God, thinking of good links us to him: our consciousness leaves the region of darkness where suffering, anxiety and terror reign and goes to rejoin the centre, the creative Principle. Since God has created everything, he knows the properties of all elements, of all forces, and of every creature in the universe, and he will give us the means to remedy our weaknesses and our shortcomings.

The universe is vast, immense and infinite in its diversity, and we cannot know everything. But the Creator is all-knowing and all-powerful, and it is thus to him that we must turn for help, for he alone is above good and evil.

17 December

*H*uman beings are inhabited by a multitude of entities that have been charged by cosmic Intelligence to watch over their development. If, through negligence or unwillingness, people are destroying something in their mind, heart, or physical body, some of these entities begin to prick and bite them to make them return to the right path.

These calls to order are what humans call suffering, and as suffering is unpleasant, they see it as an enemy. But they are wrong! On the contrary, since suffering is a warning, they must consider it to be a friend: it comes only to show them that they have strayed from the good conditions where the path was light and open before them. They must therefore make the effort to understand its language and say to it, 'May God bless you, I have understood and will rectify my mistakes.' The moment they have understood and decide to correct things, suffering is given the order to leave them, because it has done its work, it has fulfilled its mission.

18 December

*M*ost people acknowledge that they need to live in harmony, peace and light. But when they are told what they need to do to achieve it, they become more reticent: they feel they must first taste all the pleasures, and experience everything life has to offer in order 'to know life'. How can they imagine that having wasted their physical and psychic energies on such experiences, they will be in a state to do the inner work to taste the harmony, peace and light they seek. The only thing they will be capable of will be to read a few books, from which they will then quote, 'Moses said ... Buddha said ... Jesus said ...'without being able to put any of this into practice.

Well, I recommend that you first live the teaching of the great masters and that when it comes to impassioned adventures, you confine yourself to reading. The universal literature is there to teach you what human passions are. All you have to do is read, no need to have many costly experiences to find out about them. There is one life that should be lived and another that should serve simply for reading and as... a source of quotations.

19 December

*I*t is not always easy to concentrate your mind in prayer and unite with God. So do not become discouraged and impatient. Instead, try to use the following method: imagine, far away in space, a living, vibrating centre emitting rays of light radiating in all directions to nourish the celestial entities and the many creatures in the universe. This image will direct your thoughts towards the place where the divine presence manifests itself most intensely and you will feel that your prayer is echoed.

The initiates and the great masters are in constant contact with this centre of light and their thoughts generate power currents in the invisible with which we can associate ourselves so that we may feel in communion with the Lord.

20 December

*T*o show an interest in and an understanding of the various forms of spirituality is perfectly acceptable. What is dangerous, however, is to dissipate oneself, to fail to choose one method of inner work in which to engage oneself. The question is not whether we should be Catholic, Protestant, Orthodox, Muslim, Buddhist, Taoist, or nothing at all. The point – and it concerns each one of us, whether we believe or not – is to settle on a few essential spiritual truths and put them into practice.

Spirituality is not an optional realm that we can choose or not, as we do with other disciplines such as languages, art, sports, and so on. Given the structure of human beings, spirituality is a vital necessity for them. Until they become conscious of this necessity, they throw themself into activities that are useless and dangerous, both for themself and for others. Their structure is such that they need to find daily nourishment for their soul and their spirit.

21 December

In order to meet the needs of their family, some fathers are forced to leave and work abroad to earn money. Although it may appear as if they are abandoning their family, they do this to help them, and it requires great courage for them to make such decisions. And when they return, what joy the family experiences!

Let us transpose this example onto the spiritual plane. A real father, and a real mother understand that they must 'abandon' their family every day for at least a few moments in order to 'go abroad', which means to meditate, to pray, to reach the divine world where they will gain wealth. And when they return, the whole family will benefit. Contrary to what many people think, to love one's family does not mean to keep one's thought constantly fixed upon it. This is not what true love is. What does this sort of love bring in? Not very much... Those who really love their family consecrate a few moments, as often as possible, in order to unite with heaven, because they know that this link will bring true wealth to their family.

22 December

Spring, summer, autumn and winter – each season corresponds to events in our psychic life, and it is winter that symbolizes life's difficulties. In winter, all the forces in plant life descend and concentrate in the roots where they carry out a great work. The roots correspond to the subconscious in us. In winter, that is in periods of difficulty, suffering or solitude, our forces withdraw inside us, into our subconscious. But they do not remain inactive.

To live in winter is certainly difficult, but it is during winter that spring is prepared; soon everything will turn green and blossom again. We must simply be patient and wait for the currents to rise once again into our consciousness and superconsciousness. But in order to facilitate this process, certain laws must be understood: during this cold period, you must neither complain, rebel, nor become discouraged, but simply light the fire within you, and blow on it to rekindle your own heart and the hearts of all other beings.

23 December

*B*reathing reveals great mysteries to those who know how accompany it with thought. Here is an exercise you can do. When you breathe air in, imagine that all the currents in space converge towards you, towards your ego which is like an imperceptible mark, the centre of an infinite circle. Then, when you breathe out, imagine you are able to expand out towards the periphery of this circle, to the end of the universe. Once again, you contract and you expand outwards. You will discover this ebb and flow that is the key to all rhythms in the universe. In becoming aware of this movement, you will enter into cosmic harmony and exchanges take place between you and the universe: when breathing in you receive elements from space, and when breathing out you in return project something of your heart and soul.

The day you understand breathing in its spiritual dimension, you will want to dedicate your entire life to breathing the light of God in, and then to sending this light out again to all beings.

24 December

In their psychic and spiritual lives, human beings are not uniquely men or women as they are on the physical plane. The mystic who contemplates divinity is like a woman who wants to receive a spark, a seed from God. He devotes himself to the light of God; he opens himself to it, changes polarity and then receives this seed in his soul. He carries it within him for a long time in order to give birth in the world to a divine child. In the spiritual realm, a man, like a woman, can conceive and give birth to a child. In the same way, if a woman devotes herself to the service of God also learns to change polarity, she becomes active and emissive; through her spirit, she can unite with the universal Soul and give it form.

There are no barren marriages in the spiritual life, but only on the condition that men and women may learn about the laws of polarity.

25 December

What do we celebrate at Christmas? The union of the soul and spirit. They unite to give birth to a seed which is the beginning of a new consciousness within us. This consciousness manifests as an inner light that dispels all darkness, just like heat of such intensity that, even if the whole world abandons us, we never feel alone, like an abundant life that bursts forth wherever our feet take us. This consciousness is also accompanied by an influx of forces that we wish to consecrate to the edification and construction of the kingdom of God. At the same time, we also discover the extraordinary joy of feeling ourselves connected to the whole universe and to all evolved souls, of being part of this immensity, and we are certain that no one can take this joy from us.

In India, this state is called buddhic consciousness, and the Christians call it the birth of Christ.

26 December

*E*very day we must work to make our lives purer and more intense, for it is this life which will work the highest form of magic on our hearts, souls and minds, on the entities and the forces of nature, and even on physical objects.

What good does it serve to come to earth and lead a mediocre life? To eat, drink, sleep, work a little to earn a living, and have a few amorous adventures from which to emerge more or less shattered – what is all this compared to an eternity of splendour which awaits those who learn just one thing: how to live? If initiates are balanced, happy and at peace, it is because they have worked to purify their lives, and to render them beautiful and powerful. They have understood that true magic is found in life itself and nowhere else. Yes, to be able to live and breathe the divine life, to encourage others, to stimulate then, to reawaken them and ennoble them is the highest form of magic there is.

27 December

*I*f you place a metal or glass pipe above a flame, the heated air will vibrate and produce a sound. And depending on the length of the pipe, the sound emitted is lower or higher. Well, by analogy, we can say that the same phenomenon exists in human beings. Because we too are made of pipes: the spinal cord, throat, oesophagus, intestines, arteries, veins, the nervous system, and so on. And again these pipes can be longer or shorter. When the flame that burns within us – meaning the fire that keeps us alive – passes through these pipes, an extraordinary music is heard, similar to the great pipe organs in cathedrals.

A human being thus emits sounds in space and they can be heard and picked up by other beings. Obviously, if this vital energy is not equitably distributed in all the organs of the body, or if it is blocked, a terrible cacophony will result. But I am not really talking about the physical plane. It is mostly on the psychic plane that it is important for humans to succeed in organizing, purifying and enlightening their lives, and then their whole being will emit harmonious sounds. It will be such a symphony that angels and archangels will draw near to listen and be filled with wonder.

28 December

*T*he Creator has left his creatures free, and it is their responsibility to understand the direction they must follow in order to find peace, joy and the light. You will say, 'But why? Wouldn't it be better if God imposed himself on human beings and dictated the behaviour?' No, it is they who must make some efforts to understand where their interest lies and become conscious of the reason for choosing such and such a direction or making one choice rather than another. They have to be truly convinced, otherwise they will be like the cattle that the ploughman spurs to force them to plough perfectly straight furrows.

What would we gain if we were pushed against our will to follow the path of the good and light? Not much, and we would constantly have to start everything over again. That is why the Creator and celestial spirits leave human beings free; it is they who must understand and feel which path is the best for them.

29 December

*I*t is said in the *Book of Zohar* that the face of the first human was identical to that of the Creator. Later on, when the spirit of rebellion had awakened in them (a process symbolized by the serpent wrapped around the Tree of Knowledge of Good and Evil), they left Paradise where they had lived in the light. They descended into the denser regions of matter where they experienced cold, darkness, sickness and death, and their faces changed.

Now that they are no longer the faithful image of God, human beings have lost their power. The spirits of nature no longer obey them and instead take pleasure in tormenting them. But they must strive to find this primordial face again and, when they do, all the spirits of the universe will submit to them once more. Until then they will continue to resemble the prodigal son of the Gospel parable who, having left his father's house to travel the world, ends wretchedly as a swineherd. But this prodigal son finally concludes that he should return to his father's house. And one day humans will also finally understand that they must return to the Source – to the light, love and life of the heavenly Father – in order to rediscover their true face.

*D*o not wait for the kingdom of God as you would a political or social organisation that comes to impose itself on earth. The kingdom of God is first and foremost a state of consciousness, a way of living and working. That is why it cannot be realised on the physical plane until it is first realised in our thoughts. Once realised in our thoughts it will descend into the heart, into our feelings, and it is then that it can finally be expressed in our actions. For such is the order of manifestation in matter: thought – feeling – action.

One day the kingdom of God will manifest tangibly on earth, but first it must enter the thoughts and feelings of human beings. And we can see that the process has already begun. Thousands of men and women in the world nourish within themselves the ideal and love of the kingdom of God; there are many more than you may think. And in some of them, in their conduct and their way of life, the kingdom of God has in fact already come about; and even if we don't know them, it is with them that we are working.

31 December

*B*ecause they put money in the bank, buy stocks and shares, take out life insurance, and so on, many people think they are working for their future! But what do they call the future? Human beings' real future is not the thirty, forty, or fifty years they have yet to spend on earth, or even the duration of their children's and grandchildren's lives. This future for which they believe they are preparing themselves is too near because it will so soon be their present, and this present will soon become their past. Thus, their work is a waste of time.

All the events that will unfold in your current lifetime still belong to the present. This future you need to think of creating is infinity, eternity.

The Night of Wesak

*E*ach year, in the Himalayas, during the night of the full moon in May, the ceremony of Wesak takes place.*

The full moon in May is doubly under the influence of Taurus: the sun has been in this sign since 21 April, and the moon is also exalted in this sign.** Taurus represents prolific nature, fertility and abundance, emphasized further by the fact that it is the home of Venus, the planet of creation. So the full moon in May offers the best conditions for working with the forces of nature to attract heaven's blessings for the harvest and livestock, but also for human beings. For, if humans know how to attract the beneficial effects circulating through the cosmos at this time, they too can benefit from them, not only on the physical plane but also on the spiritual plane. This is why, by means of meditations, prayers, chants and magical invocations, initiates seek to create lines of force in space that will attract energies, which they send to all beings who are vigilant, awakened and capable of participating at this event.

* Wesak is the festival of the Buddha. In Tibet, it is celebrated in the valley of Wesak.

** Some years, when the sun is in Taurus, the full moon takes place in April.

There are places on earth that are more favourable than others for this cosmic work. The site where the ceremony of Wesak takes place is the most powerful of all. Some initiates go there physically, others by astral projection. But it is possible for everyone, including you, to take part in thought. During this night, you must not keep any metal object on you, since metal is not a good conductor of the waves of energy that come down from spiritual regions. But the only truly essential condition for being admitted to this festival is harmony. So be careful not to hold onto any negative thought or feeling towards others, and find the right inner attitude that will allow you to receive the blessings that the initiates send to the children of God on this night.

INDEX

A

Achievements, of spirit
- only they can truly transform life, 23 July.

Air
- feeds the fire of life, 17 Jan.

Alchemical work
- know how to suffer to become a creator, 28 April.

'And this is life eternal, that they may know You, the only true God.'
- a commentary, 7 Aug.

Angel of air
- a prayer, 27 July.

Artificial paradise
- testifies to the needs of the soul deprived of its true food, 18 April.

Artist
- must see themselves as material for their creation, 24 Oct.

Asceticism
- is not necessarily proof of spirituality, 5 Feb.

Atheism
- only considers the superficial side of beings and things, 15 Oct.

B

Balance
- a moment-to-moment victory over opposing forces, 23 Jan.

Bank
- analogy with human beings, 5 March.

Be Measured
- to preserve good relations with others, 3 Feb.

Beauty
- its relationship to kindness, 12 Dec.

Beneficial changes
- will not last unless we work on the causes, 6 May.

Birds
- symbol of a spiritual person, 2 June.

Birth of Christ
- the birth of a new consciousness in human beings, 25 Dec.

Black magic
- how to consider it, 3 June.

Blood
- is condensed light, 11 Jan.

Book of nature, the
- is the true Bible, 4 Feb.

Breathing
- a means to contact the spiritual world, 20 Sept.
- extracting the most energy possible from air, 4 Nov.
- entering into cosmic harmony, 23 Dec.

Breathing, human
- and breathing of the cosmos, 29 Aug.

Brotherhood
- is the value of the future, 9 Oct.

Building your house on a rock
- the meaning of this evangelical parable, 20 Nov.

C

Cells of our body
- a populace which observes and imitates us, 22 June.

Centres of Light
- which form a link between heaven and earth, 4 Jan.

Centres, subtle
- enable us to orientate ourselves in the spiritual world, 1 Aug.

Changes in mentality
- can resolve the problems of a society, 24 Sept.

Chaos to harmony, from
- the law of creation, 17 Aug.

Charity
- rediscover the original meaning of this word, 15 Feb.

Children
- their subconscious education, 21 April.
- their incarnation into a family is never by chance, 11 May.

Choice of a profession
- elements which determine our choice, 16 Sept.

Circle, the
- centre and periphery, spirit and matter, 1 July.

Clairvoyance
- is acquired through love, 17 June.

Clouds, Our inner
- hide the divinity, 21 Aug.

Collectivity
- it is in the interest of each individual to work for it, 13 May.

Comparing oneself
- to higher beings in order to progress, 23 Sept.

Concentration
- necessary to focus your energies, 22 Oct.

Conditions
- accept those that destiny places before us, 1 April.

Conflicts
- often originate in a trivial event, 12 June.

Conflicts with others
- resolve them by provoking their positive side, 24 July.

Consideration
- for people and for things, and how it influences us, 5 Dec.

Convictions
- do not expose them in order to better preserve them, 4 Sept.

Correct attitude, the
- to find God, 26 July.

Cosmic forces
- humans must seek how to obtain their intervention, 13 Nov.

Cosmic harmony
- an endless progression of forces, elements and beings, 3 Jan.

D

Daily tensions
- an exercise to overcome them, 16 Nov.

Dangers
- that threaten humanity, 16 March.

Descent into matter
- was foreseen by Cosmic Intelligence, 17 May.

Desire to know
- is not without risks, 18 Feb.

Desires
- questions to ask about their nature and their fulfilment, 21 Jan.

Difficulties
- do not magnify them in advance, 14 June.
- don't run away from them, train yourself to endure them, 11 Aug.

Dinosaurs to birds
- an analogy with the evolution of human beings, 20 Jan.

Diploma, the
- we receive after passing the tests of life, 28 Aug.

Discouragement
- methods to overcome it, 11 Nov.

Distress and torment
- how to avoid these states. The example of birds., 28 Sept.

Divine blessings
- open yourself in order to reveive them, 17 March.

Divine glory
- a light into which we can enter, 19 Aug.

Divine Heritage
- only this can fulfil us, 26 June.

Divine idea, A
- living entity which shapes and nourishes us, 10 Jan.

Divine intervention
- avoid asking for it when we can do something ourselves, 6 Oct.

Divine laws
- those who transgress them, limits themselves, 11 Sept.

Divine justice
- takes into account what we do with the faculties we are given, 27 Jan.
- its manifestations, 16 July.

Divine will
- attune one's projects to it, 10 Nov.

Divine wisdom
- trust it, because it has foreseen everything for our evolution, 9 Jan.

Divinity
- a spiritual master works on the Divinity that lives within each being, 31 Jan.

Division
- its dangers, 14 July.

Doubt
- makes us vulnerable, 2 Feb.

E

Eat fire and drink light, 26 April.

Efforts
- technical progress should not exempt us from making efforts, 25 Oct.
- alone can take us closer to God, 3 Nov.

Egregor
- definition and activity, 29 Sept.

Emanations, human
- are used by heavenly entities, 17 July.

Errors
- Cosmic Intelligence allows us the time to correct them, 11 April.

Essence of life
- is to be found within, 21 Feb.

Evil
- the perception we have of it is very relative, 8 June.
- by giving too much importance to it, human beings only reinforce it, 5 July.
- its power comes from human beings, 14 Oct.

Evolution
- occurs when the conditions are favourable, 12 Feb.

Evolution, our
- depends on the stimulation we receive from the physical, psychic and spiritual realms, 10 Dec.

Exchanges
- we make with nature and all beings must be more profound, 20 April.

Experiences
- which you must favour, 18 Dec.

Experiments
- to be performed before stating conclusions, 3 March.

F

Face, our
- bears the reflection of what we seek in others, 6 Feb.

Failures
- lessons to be learned, 29 May.

Faith
- founded on an experience of the divine world, 4 May.
- whatever is sown bears fruit, 11 June.
- knowledge based on experience, 15 Sept.

Faith and Belief, 1 March.

Faith and doubt
- chemical elements which favour fulfilment or oppose it, 7 Sept.

Faith in good
- enables us to conquer fear, 19 Sept.

Falling in love
- learning to expand your consciousness, 30 July.

Family
- must not be understood as a goal, but as a point of departure, 13 March.

Fate, our
- is determined by our attitude to the divine world, 24 Nov.

Fear
- the only legitimate fear is that of transgressing the divine order, 18 Jan.
- is conquered by the light, 19 Oct.

Feeling
- is the only reality for humans, 29 March.
- gives us more of an understanding of reality than seeing, 18 Sept.

Field of consciousness
- broadens when we contemplate immensity, 23 June.

Fire and air
- represented within us by love and wisdom, 29 Jan.

Flowers
- have a voice we can hear, 22 May.
- an image of human beings of which we should only smell the scent, 22 July.

Food
- talks to us when we are silent, 30 June.

Force
- its use does not resolve problems, 15 March.

Forces of evil
- always awaken the rise of forces of good, 8 Dec.

Freedom
- work in the present to create the future, 28 Jan.
- its condition: always place the spirit first, 10 April.
- begins with mastering oneself, 18 Aug.

Freedom of movement
- physically and psychically it depends on our vigilance, 8 Nov.

From Caterpillar to Butterfly
- the process of evolution, 15 May.

Happiness
- depends on the way in which we organise our inner world, 6 Sept.

Hardship
- accept the idea that it is helpful for our evolution, 20 June.

Hardships
- learning to overcome them, 2 July.
- accept them but do not look for them, 13 July.
- how to consider your own and those of others, 3 Oct.

Harm
- comes more from ourselves than from others, 29 April.

Harmony
- attracts heavenly entities, 21 March.
- a collective work for the kingdom of God, 5 May.
- its effects on health, 10 July.

Hate
- never use God to justify it, 23 April.

Heart, mind, will
- take care only to give away their fruits, 25 April.

Heaven
- is for those who have worked, 13 Dec.

Heavenly Father and divine Mother
- never forget that we are their children, 11 Feb.

Heavenly homeland, our
- its memory lives within us, 6 April.

Help
- we obtain more through our light than recounting our misfortunes, 16 Jan.

Helping others
- is never wasted, 12 Sept.

Higher self
- release the spiritual energies needed to feed it, 19 April.
- how to rejoin it, 31 Aug.

Holy pictures
- are only the point of departure for prayer, 29 Oct.

Hope
- a foretaste of perfection, 22 March.
- is maintained through faith and love, 7 July.

Hope, faith and love
- form, content and meaning, 13 Jan.

Host
- its symbolic value is strengthened by the attitude of the faithful, 13 April.

Human body, the
- a model for the body of the world, 1 Sept.
- an analogy with the great pipe organs in cathedrals, 27 Dec.

Human life
- the interval between the first and final breaths, 2 Jan.

Human marriage
- reproduces a cosmic phenomenon, 15 July.

Humility
- preserves us from the snares of the lower nature, 1 Feb.
- analogy with the universal solvent of alchemists, 26 Aug.

I

Ideas and opinions
- revise them and sort through them, 15 Aug.

Identification with God
- how to understand this exercise, 8 May.

Identifying
- being able to merge with all that exists, 2 Aug.

'If you have faith like a mustard seed'
- comment, 26 Feb.

Ignorance
- is never an excuse, 10 Aug.

Imagination
- a screen on which the realities of the invisible world are projected, 24 April.
- a power which must be directed, 13 Sept.

In the Soul and the Spirit
- will be found the only riches which are ours forever, 14 April.

Incarnation, each
- must prepare us for the next, 21 May.

Incense, burning
- the symbolic meaning, 8 Feb.

Initiatic school
- is beneficial only to the development of our divine nature, 31 July.

Initiatic Science
- must not serve materialists, 17 Nov.

Initiations
- their goal: to unite spirit and matter, 7 June.

Inner flame
- strengthen it so that no breath can extinguish it, 20 May.

Inner silence
- where we discover another dimension of time and space, 7 Jan.

Inner tribunal
- rely only on its judgement, 27 Nov.

Inner view
- get rid of everything which obscures it, 5 Oct.

Inner winters
- that we need to prepare ourselves for, 29 Nov.

Inspiration
- the conditions for it to pay us a visit, 17 Oct.

Intelligence
- depends on the food we take in on all planes, 25 June.

Intuition
- is both understanding and feeling, 25 Nov.

Invisible world
- unconsciously, it is the realities of the Invisible world to which we attach the greatest importance, 19 June.

J

'Just as I have loved you, you also should love one another'
- an interpretation, 28 Oct.

K

Kindness
- one of the highest forms of intelligence, 30 Sept.

Kingdom of God
- let us all stand together to claim it, 16 Aug.
- is firstly a state of consciousness, 30 Dec.

'Know thyself'
- significance of this concept, 12 March.

Knowledge
- is power, 13 June.

Knowledge, True
- is an acquisition of the inner life, 5 Aug.

L

Language of initiates
- is identical to that of nature, 25 July.

Last Sacraments, the
- their role, 2 Nov.

Laws
- rule the psychic world as they rule the physical world, 11 July.

Laws of economics
- are also valid in the spiritual world, 14 Feb.

Life
- is sustained within us by the entities that populate the universe, 8 Jan.
- its forms and manifestations are limitless, 20 March.
- only belongs to God, for he is life, 11 Dec.

Life and Death
- always co-exist, 7 Dec.

Life of Nature
- make contact with it, 22 Sept.

Light
- alone gives real power and knowledge, 21 July.

Likes and dislikes
- are not reliable criteria, 2 Oct.

Likings
- should be moderated and guided, 2 May.

Lineage, our divine
- an exercise to recognise it, 28 July.

Loneliness
- how to overcome it, 13 Aug.

Lord's visit, the
- can only take place in a comfortable house, 18 Nov.

Lose control
- to break the connection with heaven, 10 Oct.

Love
- a quality of divine life, 19 Jan.
- save it by devoting it to God, 26 Jan.
- its source is within us, 25 Feb.
- protect it by keeping your distance, 24 March.
- two opposite images; a wood stove and the sun, 10 May.
- must be lived in joy and light, 31 May.
- without expecting anything, 10 June.
- a state of consciousness, 27 June.
- the intellect should have just as much to say as the heart, 3 Aug.
- the transformations it produces within us, 25 Aug.
- it makes us light and brings us closer to heaven, 3 Sept.
- that we give each other enriches us, 9 Sept.
- maintaining the poetic nature of its beginnings, 21 Oct.

Love and hate
- manifestations of the same force on two different planes, 19 Nov.

Love for one's family
- go and find nourishment in the divine world, 21 Dec.

Love God
- in order to love human beings better, 18 Oct.

'Love your enemies'
- a commentary, 21 Sept.

Lower nature
- distrusting it should inspire us, 22 April.

M

'Make humankind in our image'
- interpretation, 13 Feb.

Mantras
- saying them out loud, 23 Oct.

Marriage
- in the spiritual life there is never a sterile marriage, 24 Dec.

Mastering ourdestiny
- do not count on anything that comes from the outside, 25 March.

Meaning
- give one's life a richer and richer meaning, 30 Jan.

Method, A
- needs to be found for each new problem, 6 Jan.

Miracles
- obey the laws of Nature, 19 Feb.

Moments of abundance
- think of sharing them with the whole world, 5 Jan.

Music
- how to use it in your spiritual work, 6 July.
- importance of the feelings it generates, 24 Aug.

Music of the spheres
- those who vibrate in harmony with the universe can hear it, 14 Sept.

'My Father is still working, and I also am working'
- commentary, 26 May.

N

Nature
- is alive and intelligent, 2 Sept.

Needs
- direct them to the spiritual level where the possibilities are infinite, 20 Oct.
- adults must reflect on the needs they awaken in young people, 15 Dec.

Negative states
- method to overcome them, 10 March.

New Year
- start it with blessings, 1 Jan.

Noise and silence
- their affinities with childhood and old-age, 8 Sept.

Nutrition and breathing
- chew air like we would food, 4 Oct.

O

Obstacles
- we overcome them by rising up to our higher self, 6 Dec.

Old age
- period when we taste the fruit of our efforts, 30 Oct.

Om - Aum
- using this mantra, 15 June.

Our efforts
- necessarily produce results, 19 May.

Our faults are recorded within us
- it is not God who punishes us, 8 April.

Our higher self
- purify ourselves in order to receive its messages, 18 May.

P

Painful tasks
- consider them as beneficial exercises, 21 Nov.

Parents, our divine
- they are within us, just like our human parents, 27 Aug.

Parsifal
- symbol of the adept on the path of initiation, 2 April.

Patience
- strengthen it by breathing, 30 May.

Pentecost
- the Spirit descends upon us to the extent that we are capable of elevating ourselves, 4 June.

Perfection
- should remain a rule of life, 26 Oct.

Phycic states, our
- influence others, for which we are responsible, 5 April.

Physical and spiritual planes
- there is no separation between them, 22 Jan.

Pleasure
- does not constitute happiness, 14 Aug.

Points of view
- we need to test their validity, 17 Feb.
- know how to call them into question, 13 Oct.

Powers of life
- give them the means to triumph within, 11 Oct.

Prana
- we can harness it through breathing, 12 July.

Prayer
- reaching God through our higher self, 14 Jan.
- is not about addressing grievances to God, 4 Aug.
- connecting with a centre of light, 19 Dec.

Prayers
- address them instead to entities whose task is to take care of human beings, 26 Nov.

Pregnant woman, a
- must protect her child from dark entities, 9 Nov.

Pride and humility
- one impoverishes you, the other enriches you, 4 Dec.

Problems
- forgetting them for a while helps to find a solution, 16 Oct.

Promises, made to us
- know ahead of time that they will not always be kept, 20 Aug.

Psychic emanations
- pollute or purify the air, 23 Feb.

Psychic life
- its effects on the physical body, 7 Nov.

Punishments, heavenly
- wrong beliefs, 20 July.

R

Reflecting well
- before taking action, 22 Nov.

Regenerating ourselves
- through connection with the divine source, 17 Sept.

Relations
- that we must seek to have with humans and with nature, 27 Feb.

Relationships with others
- it is important to widen and improve them, 14 Nov.

Religions
- their forms must evolve, 15 April.

Renunciation
- creating a void within that can be filled with divine virtues, 6 Nov.

Resurrection
- starts with work on life within us, 16 April.

Revenge
- don't give in to it, 30 Aug.

Right path, the
- human beings must choose it in all consciousness and freedom, 28 Dec.

S

Sacrifice
- source of life and joy, 22 Feb.

Sagittarius
- its symbolism: instincts put to the service of an ideal, 14 Dec.

Salvation
- is in the divine imprint that humans carry within, 27 Oct.

Scent
- given off by the virtuous attracts celestial entities, 7 May.

Scepticism
- is an arrogant and pretentious attitude, 24 June.

Scientists
- and their contradictions, 27 May.

Security
- seek it in the world of the soul and spirit, 12 Nov.

Self-doubt
- how to conquer it, 3 Dec.

Sensitivity
- is dulled by excess, 17 April.
- be able to open yourself to the riches of the divine world, 25 May.

Serpent to dove
- sublimation of sexual energy, 3 May.

Sexual energy
- why make the effort to bring it under control, 19 July.

Sexual force
- 'the most powerful force of all forces', 5 June.

Silence
- an expression of divine presence, 27 March.
- place of fulfilment and perfect movement, 9 May.
- enables us to fuse with the light, 18 July.

Skin
- what we receive through it is determined by our thoughts and feelings, 23 Aug.

Solar light
- receive it and project it, 9 Aug.

Solutions, real
- are only found on high, in the domain of the spirit, 29 July.

Soul and spirit
- the importance of the events taking place at this level, 26 Sept.
- you need to relate to in others, 30 March.

Soul mate
- we attract them by living a luminous life, 27 Sept.

Source of life
- always remain connected to it, 3 April.

Spirit, the
- a summit from which we have all the opportunities to take action, 10 Feb.

Spiritual brotherhood
- its benefits, 22 Aug.

Spiritual commitment
- once made it must be kept, 1 Oct.

Spiritual Exercises
- enable us to resonate with spirits of light, 8 Aug.

Spiritual guide
- false pretexts for refusing the idea of it, 9 Feb.
- danger of trying to be one if you have not received the qualification, 12 Aug.

Spiritual master
- their only obligation: guiding us on the path of the light, 15 Nov.

Spiritual practices
- help us rediscover light and love, 31 Oct.

Spiritual riches
- only these are inexhaustible, 6 March.

Spiritual royalty
- implies mastery of self, 1 June.

Spirituality
- vital necessity for human beings, 20 Dec.

Stale air to clean air
- a change in philosophy, 11 March.

Subtle life
- create a relationship with the subtle life of beings, 25 Sept.

Suffering
- pray only that it will help us grow, 16 Feb.
- Cosmic Intelligence only inflicts it as a last resort, 19 March.
- accepted with love produces a perfume, 29 June.
- its role is to give us warnings, 17 Dec.

Sun
- visit it with our soul and spirit, 12 April.

- learn to be like it by projecting light and love, 21 June.
- as we open ourselves to it, so we must open to God, 8 July.
- gives the principles of a universal religion, 10 Sept.

Sunrise
- repetition of the first morning of the world, 23 March.

T

Take stock of life
- do not wait too long to do it, 4 April.

Talisman
- its powers depend on us. The Pentagram. 1 May.

Thank you
- magical words capable of transforming everything, 12 Jan.

The Causal Plane
- region of stability and security, 14 March.

The five senses
- what they can teach us about the people we meet, 27 April.

The heart and the intellect
- must be balanced, 18 March.

The occult
- its dangers for those who break the laws of cosmic harmony, 28 June.

The sun
- helps us find our own center, 28 May.

The tongue
- is responsible for many events in our lives, both happy and unhappy, 16 May.

Third lodge, the, 23 Nov.

Thought
- its role in our perfection, 8 March.
- can strengthen the effect of medication, 3 July.

Thoughts
- living and active entities, 25 Jan.
- are children we are responsible for, 6 June.
- their creative power, 7 Oct.

Thoughts and feelings
- are like talismans that can attract or ward off influences, 28 Nov.

'To know, to want, to dare, to be silent'
- Why be silent?, 26 March.

Traces
- that we leave wherever we go, 12 May.

Tree
- symbol of what humans are capable of giving, 7 April.

Trees
- consider them as living beings, 18 June.

Trowel and sword
- the symbolic meaning of these two masonic symbols, 5 Nov.

True face
- we will rediscover it when we return to the house of the father, 29 Dec.

True magic
- live and breathe the divine life, 26 Dec.

Truth
- we will never be able to reach it, 24 Feb.
- we find it as we perfect ourselves, 9 July.

Truth about beings and things
- only through intuition can it be known, 14 May.

U

Unity
- should exclude nothing and no-one, 4 March.

Universal life
- in which we must participate consciously, 24 May.
- it is in this direction that we must strive, 16 June.

Use kindness the foundation of your life
- a rule from Master Peter Deunov, 23 May.

V

Virtues
- seeds which grow in the spiritual sun, 28 March.

Voice of heaven
- talks to us softly, 24 Jan.

Voice of silence, the
- conditions to be able to hear it, 30 Nov.

W

Waves
- from celestial regions; learning to capture them, 2 March.

'When you pray, go into your room'
- a commentary, 9 Dec.

Winter
- what it represents in our psychic life, 22 Dec.

Woman
- educator of man, 28 Feb.

Women
- how they can contribute to the regeneration of humankind, 6 Aug.

Work
- whatever the conditions may be, 1 Dec.

Work, time and faith
- conditions for success, 1 Nov.

Y

Youthfulness
- a quality of the soul, 20 Feb.

Note: The three fundamental activities which characterize human beings are thinking (by means of the intellect or mind), feeling (by means of the heart), and doing (by means of the physical body). You must not believe that only the physical body is material; the heart and mind are also material instruments, but the matter of which they are made is far subtler than that of the physical body.

HIGHER NATURE

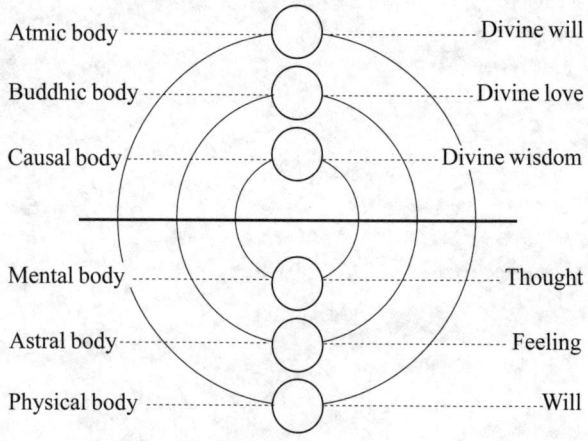

Atmic body	Divine will
Buddhic body	Divine love
Causal body	Divine wisdom
Mental body	Thought
Astral body	Feeling
Physical body	Will

LOWER NATURE

An age-old esoteric tradition teaches that the support or vehicle of feeling is the astral body, and that of the intellect, the mental body. But this trinity made up of our physical, astral, and mental bodies, constitutes our imperfect human nature, and the three faculties of thought, feeling, and action also exist on a higher level, their vehicles being respectively, the causal, buddhic, and atmic bodies which go to make up our divine self.

In the diagram, the three large concentric circles indicate the links which exist between the lower and the higher bodies. The physical body, which represents strength, will, and power on the material level, is linked to the atmic body, which represents divine power, strength, and will. The astral body, which represents our egotistical, personal feelings and desires, is linked to the buddhic body, which represents divine love. The mental body, which represents our ordinary, self-serving thoughts, is linked to the causal body, which represents divine wisdom.

(Man's Psychic Life: Elements and Structures, Izvor Collection No. 222, chap. 3)

Introduction to the Sephirotic Tree

Jesus said, 'And this is eternal life, that they may know you, the only true God'.

For those who aspire to know the Creator of heaven and earth, to feel his presence, to enter into his infinity and his eternity, it is necessary to have a deep understanding of a system that explains the world. The system that seemed to me to be the best, the most extensive and at the same time the most precise I found in the cabbalistic tradition – the sephirotic Tree, the Tree of Life. Its knowledge offers the deepest, most structured, overall view of what we need to study and work on.

The cabbalists divide the universe into ten regions or ten sephiroth corresponding to the first ten numbers (the word 'sephirah' and its plural 'sephiroth' mean enumeration). Each sephirah is identified by means of five names: the name of God, the name of the sephirah, the name of the archangel at the head of the angelic order, the angelic order itself, and a planet. God directs these ten regions, but under a different name in each one. This is why the Cabbalah gives God ten names, each corresponding to different attributes. God is one, but manifests in a different way in each region.

This Tree of Life is presented as a very simple diagram, but its contents are inexhaustible. For me it is the key that allows the mysteries of creation to be deciphered. It is not meant to teach us astronomy or cosmology, and anyway no one can say exactly what the universe is or how it was created. This Tree represents an explanatory system of the world that is by nature mystical. Through meditation and contemplation and a life of saintliness, the exceptional minds that devised it came to grasp a cosmic reality, and it is essentially their teaching that survives to this day, passed down by tradition and continually taken up and meditated on through the centuries.

A spiritual Master is conscious of the responsibilities he is taking by allowing humans to enter this holy sanctuary, and so when you approach this knowledge you must do so with much humility, respect and reverence. By returning often to this diagram, you will find lights being switched on inside you. You will certainly never manage to explore all its riches, but from Malkuth to Kether this representation of an ideal world will always draw you higher.

TREE OF LIFE

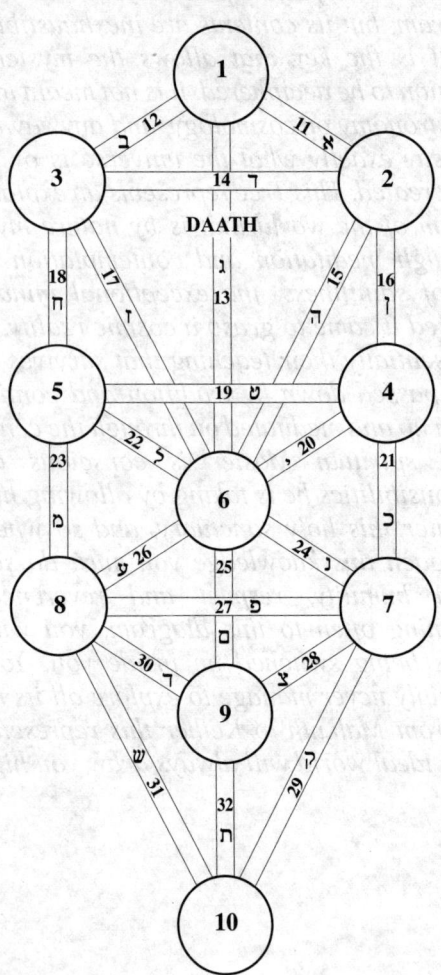

DAATH

404

TREE OF LIFE

1 Ehieh
Kether – *Crown*
Metatron
Hayoth haKadesch – *Seraphim*
Rashith haGalgalim – *First Swirlings (Neptune)*
♆

3 Jehovah
Binah – *Understanding*
Tzaphkiel
Aralim – *Thrones*
Shabbathai – *Saturn*
♄

2 Yah
Chokmah – *Wisdom*
Raziel
Ophanim – *Cherubim*
Mazloth – *The Zodiac (Uranus)*
♅

5 Elohim Gibor
Geburah – *Severity*
Kamaël
Seraphim – *Powers*
Maadim – *Mars*
♂

4 El
Chesed – *Mercy*
Tzsadkiel
Hashmalim – *Dominations*
Tzedek– *Jupiter*
♃

8 Elohim Tzebaoth
Hod – *Glory*
Raphaël
Bnei-Elohim – *Archangels*
Kokab – *Mercury*
☿

7 Jehovah Tzebaoth
Netzach – *Victory*
Haniel
Elohim – *Principalities*
Noga – *Venus*
♀

9 Shaddai El Hai
Yesod – *Foundation*
Gabriel
Kerubim – *Angels*
Levana – *Moon*
☽

6 Eloha vaDaath
Tiphareth – *Beauty*
Mikhaël
Malakhim – *Virtues*
Shemesh – *Sun*
☉

10 Adonai-Melek
Malkuth – *The Kingdom*
Uriel (Sandalfon)
Ishim – *Beatified Souls*
Olem Ha Yesodoth – *Earth*
♁

Editor-Distributor
World Wide - Editor-Distributor
Editions Prosveta S.A. - Z.A. Le Capitou - CS 30012
F - 83601 Fréjus CEDEX (France)
Tel. (33) 04 94 19 33 33 – Fax (33) 04 94 19 33 34
www.prosveta.fr – www.prosveta.com
international@prosveta.com

* Publisher in his own language - ** Distributor - *** POS

Distributors

AUSTRALIA
** PROSVETA AUSTRALIA – Port Kennedy WA 6172
Tel. (61) 8 9594 1145 – prosveta.au@aapt.net.au
CANADA
** PROSVETA Inc. – Canton-de-Hatley (Qc), J0B 2C0
Tel. (819) 564-8212 – Fax. (819) 564-1823
in Canada, call toll free: 1-800-854-8212
prosveta@prosveta-canada.com – www.prosveta-canada.com
CYPRUS
** THE SOLAR CIVILISATION BOOKSHOP. – 1305 Nicosie
Tél. 00357-22-377 503 – heavenlight@primehome.com - www.prosveta.com
GREAT BRITAIN – IRELAND
** PROSVETA – East Sussex TN 22 3JJ
Tel. (44) (01825) 712988 – Fax (44) (01825) 713386
orders@prosveta.co.uk – www.prosveta.co.uk
HOLLAND
* STICHTING PROSVETA NEDERLAND – 3871 TD Hoevelaken
Tél. (31) 33 25 345 75 – Fax. (31) 33 25 803 20
prosveta@worldonline.nl – www.prosveta.nl
INDIA
* VIJ BOOKS INDIA PVT. LTD. *(Anglais et Hindi)* – New Dehli - 110 002
Tel. + 91-11-43596460, 011-65449971 – Fax +91-11-47340674
vijbooks@rediffmail.com – www.vijbooks.com
* BOOK MEDIA (Malayalam) – Kerala
Tél. +91 94 47 53 62 40 – bookmediaindia@gmail.com
www.indulekha.com/bookmedia
ISRAEL
* HADKEREN PUBLISHING HOUSE – Tel-Aviv Jaffa 6108301
LIBAN
** PROSVETA LIBAN – P.O. Box 90-995 – Jdeidet-el-Metn, Beirut
Tél. 961 (0) 3 448 560 – prosveta_lb@terra.net.lb

NEW ZEALAND
  * PROSVETA NEW ZEALAND LTD – Gisborne
  Tel. (64) (0)9 889 0805 – port. 027 3560107
  info@prosveta.co.nz – www.prosveta.co.nz
NORWAY
  * PROSVETA Norden – N-1502 Moss
  Tel. (47) 90 27 43 33 – Fax (47) 69 20 67 60
  info@prosveta.no – www.prosveta.no
UNITED STATES
  ** Prosveta Books – M. Mendes – New York 11560
  Tel. (718) 844 0456 – Tel. (516) 674 4428
  prosvetausa@gmail.com – www.fbu-usa.com
  ** PROSVETA US Dist. – Canyon Country CA 91387
  Tel. (661) 252-9090 – prosveta@sbcglobal.net – www.prosveta-usa.com

Updated list 28.09.2015

List of editors and distributors prosveta continually updated on
www.prosveta.fr/en/prosveta-around-the-world

Printed in June 2016
by Imprimerie France Quercy
46090 Mercuès – France

Dépôt légal : Juin 2016